AI, Robots and Humans: Our Servants or Masters?

A Spiritual Perspective on Society's Coexistence with AI and Robots

Rev. Oreste J. DAversa

PUBLISHER'S NOTE

This book is designed to provide accurate and authoritative information. information in regard to the subject matter covered. It is sold with the understanding that neither the author nor publisher is engaged in rendering psychological, legal, or other professional service. If psychological, legal, professional advice or other expert assistance is required, the services of a professional in that field should be sought. The principles and concepts presented in this book are the opinions of the author and are based on his interpretations of the aforementioned principles. Neither the author nor publisher is liable or responsible to any person or entity for any errors contained on this book, or website, or for any special, incidental, or consequential damage caused or alleged to be caused directly or indirectly by the information contained on this book or website. Any application of the techniques, ideas, and suggestions in this book is at the reader's sole discretion and risk.

No part of this publication may be reproduced, redistributed, taught, stored in a retrieval system, or transmitted, in any form, or by any means, electronic, mechanical, photocopy, recording, or otherwise, without the prior written permission of the publisher.

FIRST EDITION

ISBN: 978-1-952294-29-7

Library of Congress Control Number: 2023911331

Published by: Cutting Edge Technology Publishing

Copyright © Oreste J. D'Aversa, 2023. All rights reserved.

TABLE OF CONTENTS

About the Author   5

Forward   9

Preface   13

Introduction   17

01. Exploring AI, Human, and Robot Interaction   25

02. What is AI (Artificial Intelligence)?   35

03. What is Consciousness?   41

04. What does it Mean to be a Self-Actualized Being?   45

05. What does it Mean to be a Sentient Being?   51

06. What Does it Mean to Be Human?   57

07. What Does it Mean to Be a Robot?   63

08. Comparing Humans to Robots – The Similarities and Differences   69

09. Robots – Are They Helping Us or Hurting Us?   77

10. What Happens if Things Go Right with Working with Robots?	83
11. What Happens if Things Go Wrong with Working with Robots?	89
12. Can there be a Balance between Humans and Robots Working Together?	95
13. The Wildcard: Humankind's Use of Technology for Good or Evil?	101
14. What Does the Future Hold for AI, Robots, and Humans?	107
Conclusion	113
Bibliography	119
Suggested Reading List	153

About The Author

Reverend Oreste J. DAversa (O-res-tee DA-versa) is an Interfaith (All-Faiths) Minister ordained by The New Seminary in New York City and is legally recognized as Clergy.

Informally known as **"Reverend Rusty"**, he was raised Catholic. Reverend DAversa has studied the teachings of: Jesus the Christ, many of the Prophets, the Ascended Masters, the major religions, and many spiritual practices of the world and has worked with Shamans.

He is here to serve GOD and mankind and to help make the world a better place for all people.
He is also a Spiritual Coach, Guide, and Teacher and helps people find their true life's work and their spiritual path.
You can learn more about his work as an Interfaith Minister at **www.GodLovesYouAndMe.org**

He also has over twenty years of experience in the Technology Industry (Training, Consulting, Technical Support, Pre/Post Sales Support, Front Line Sales, and Customer Service).

He also owns Metropolitan Small Business Coaching LLC (**www.MetroSmallBusinessCoaching.com**) where is a Small Business Coach, Consultant, Trainer, Author, Speaker, Seminar Leader, Public Speaking Coach, and University Lecturer.

He is a Job Search/Career Coach for new and experienced people in the workforce and also works with young people to help them find their college major at www.CollegeMajorCoaching.com.

He appears as a guest on podcasts, radio, and television discussing his expertise in business-related and personal growth subjects, and has authored numerous books, manuals, articles, and audio CDs.

Books by Rev. Oreste J. DAversa
(Available on Amazon.com):

- UNPLUGGED! A Practical Guide to Managing Teenage Stress in the Digital Age

- I Didn't Get a Chance to Say Good-bye ... Now What Can I Do?

- Write Your Own Funeral Service

- Life Beyond the Pandemic: A Practical New Journey Handbook

- Healing the Holes in My Soul!: How I Saved My Own Life, Became Whole to Lead a Happy, Fulfilling and Joyous Life!

Books by Rev. Oreste J. DAversa
(Available on Amazon.com):

- Baby Boomer Entrepreneur:
Implementing the Boomer Business Success System
The Complete and Proven Guide to Starting a Successful Business, while Making a Difference in the World!

- Selling for Non-Selling Professionals©:
Learn Basic, Proven, and Results Oriented Sales Skills, Methods and Techniques to Get Clients Consistently with No Prior Sales Background and Increase Revenue

- The Resume and Cover Letter Writing Toolkit
for the Successful Job Seeker

- Power Interviewing:
Proven Job Interview Techniques That Get You Results!

- The Step-by-Step Business Networking Kit:
The Ultimate Business Networking System that Delivers Superior Results!

- SELL More Technology NOW!
Proven Sales Methods and Established Practices that Deliver Results

- The Seven Simple Principles of Prosperity:
Practical Exercises to Achieve a Rich, Happy and Joyous Life!

THIS PAGE INTENTIONALLY LEFT BLANK

Forward

In the age of rapid technological advancement, the emergence of Artificial Intelligence (AI) and robots has left humanity standing at a crossroads, pondering the intricate dynamics of our coexistence. As we witness the transformation of our world, it becomes imperative to delve deeper, beyond the surface of algorithms and mechanics, to explore the spiritual dimensions of this profound journey.

"AI, Robots and Humans: Our Servants or Masters? A Spiritual Perspective on Society's Coexistence with AI and Robots" invites us to embark on an extraordinary exploration, where the realms of spirituality and technology converge. Within these pages, we navigate the uncharted territories of our evolving relationship with AI and robots, guided by the light of spiritual wisdom.

In a world that often emphasizes the external aspects of progress, it is crucial to remember that technology, at its core, is a reflection of the human mind and spirit. As we embark on this quest, let us peel away the layers of silicon and steel to uncover the spiritual essence that permeates our technological advancements. By doing so, we open ourselves to profound insights that transcend the boundaries of scientific understanding alone.

Throughout this book, we will embark on a journey of self-discovery and contemplation, inviting us to question the very nature of our existence. What does it mean to be conscious? What is the essence of being human? How do we define our relationship with AI and robots, and how can spirituality shed light on this complex interplay?

We will explore the realms of consciousness, self-actualization, and sentience, seeking to unravel the intricate tapestry that connects us all. Through a spiritual lens, we will inquire into the potential of AI and robots to mirror aspects of our own consciousness, inviting us to reflect on the profound mysteries of our existence.

As we navigate the chapters that follow, we will encounter thought-provoking questions and profound insights. We will examine the implications of our choices as we interact with AI and robots, recognizing the tremendous power we hold to shape the future. Let us not lose sight of the moral and ethical considerations that come with this responsibility.

Furthermore, we will explore the potential for harmony and balance between humans and technology. Can we create a symbiotic relationship where AI and robots serve as allies in our spiritual and societal growth? What lessons can we learn from the wisdom traditions of the past, where humanity lived in harmony with the natural world?

As we embark on this spiritual odyssey, let us approach these questions with humility and an open heart. Let us cultivate a deep reverence for the interconnectedness of all beings and embrace the opportunity for collective transformation that lies before us. Together, we can weave a future where AI and robots become catalysts for the evolution of our consciousness and the realization of our highest human potential.

May this book serve as a guiding light, illuminating our path toward a future where technology and spirituality converge. May it inspire us to foster a profound sense of responsibility, compassion, and reverence for life as we navigate the uncharted territories of this evolving relationship.

Now, dear reader, let us embark on this transformative journey, where spirituality and technology intertwine, and where we seek to understand the delicate dance between AI, robots, and humans. May the insights gained from this exploration guide us toward a future where our coexistence fosters harmony, growth, and the flourishing of the human spirit.

Thank you for the privilege of your time in reading this book.

THIS PAGE INTENTIONALLY LEFT BLANK

Preface

As AI and robotics continue to expand at skyrocketing rates my concern as an Interfaith Minister is that the rest of human development is not growing as well, and/or at the same rate as our technology development. This leads me to the conclusion that if humankind only excels on the physical plane of existence that creates an "out-of-balance" condition to the other aspect of a human being's existence, that is, the mental, emotional, and spiritual aspects of being human.

The purpose of this book is to educate the reader on what AI and robots are and the advantages and disadvantages of working with both in our human society, what will be the cost to humankind, and what may be the spiritual cost to society and humans if AI and robot technology grow without any type of ethical controls monitoring them both.

Modern-day humankind seems to negate, for the most part, that we are made of 4 major components of our existence – the physical, the mental, the emotional, and the spiritual. If any one of these aspects incurs a major out-of-balance situation then "dis-ease" is created in the human condition which for the most part manifests itself in negative ways to humankind. This book has been written to be mindful of this principle in the hopes that AI and robots will be used to better the quality of life for all humankind.

Having worked in the technology industry for 20 years, and now using technology on a daily basis, and being an Interfaith Minister I am uniquely qualified to discuss these matters and the various facets associated with each. While this book is not here to decide what is right or wrong about AI and robots it is going to be a forum to educate and discuss the advantages and disadvantages of these technologies to modern-day life and their effects on society.

Having seen firsthand how technology has impacted the workforce in modern-day life with many people losing jobs because of new technologies being introduced and conversely many new jobs and opportunities being created by new technologies. The negative impact is that many people in the workplace are treated like the technology they work with, being treated as obsolete once the use for the technology and services that are associated with it are no longer needed and both in essence being "kicked to the curb" as though they were an old, ineffective and useless, like an old vacuum cleaner. A classic example is computer card machines and the computer card punch operators that worked them, both are no longer in existence due to more efficient means of data entry to computers.

AUTHOR DISCLOSURE

As an Inter-Faith Minister, business person, and a person with ethical standards I believe in being transparent with the readers of this book. I am far from perfect as a human being nor do I pretend to be, there are certain financial realities that are the "facts of life' in surviving, prospering, and helping others in modern-day life. The bank that holds my house mortgage does not care how many people I have helped, nor do they care how many people I have gotten through various crises or the personal relationship I have with the famous Prophet (Jesus the Christ) that walked the earth over 2,000 years ago.

Having been formally, informally, and self-taught in the areas of computers, technology, and associated work areas. I have been taught the following: computers basically do 2 things – they store vast amounts of information (data) and they do calculations extremely fast.

A third thing that is now being added to this teaching is Artificial Intelligence (AI). Now there is the opportunity for meaningful interaction with computers, the technology behind them, and robotics. It is my personal belief that if there are no human beings behind the above all there is, is a metal box of printed circuit boards, hard drives, and software instructions. This leads to the following discloser as the author of this book it is my thoughts that have created and have driven this book.

My thoughts, coming from my mind and consciousness, have formulated the thoughts speculations, and theories that are being presented through this medium to the reader. With that said I am disclosing that part of this book has been written using AI. While an author is not obligated to disclose if they used AI in writing their book. I have chosen to disclose this information as a way of being transparent about my writing process and giving credit to the AI technology used. What chapters/areas are inconsequential, as all the foundational thinking comes directly from me, my mind, and my consciousness. AI here is just being used here to expedite the writing of this book to bring it to the marketplace faster.

Also, truth be told, I will be 64 years old this year, the initial printing of this book. Should the using of AI in the writing of this book be an issue for the reader I completely understand and I am confident that wherever you have purchased this book will refund your money.

Furthermore, it is my personal belief, that as an individual if you're not the "sharpest pencil in the box", computers, AI, and robots are not going to miraculously "make you any sharper".

Introduction

In a world where technology rapidly advances, artificial intelligence (AI) and robots have become an integral part of our lives. They assist us in various domains, from enhancing productivity to performing complex tasks. As we witness this ever-evolving relationship between humans and machines, it is crucial to explore the profound implications and ramifications of this coexistence. There will be an examination of various topics, concepts, and ideas in this book on how they all relate to AI, robots, and human beings. Below is a summary of the book that will begin your journey:

Chapter 1: Exploring AI, Human, and Robot Interaction
In this beginning chapter, we embark on a journey to delve into the intricate dynamics of AI, human, and robot interaction. We will investigate the profound questions that arise as we navigate the boundaries between technology and humanity. By embracing a spiritual perspective, we seek to uncover insights that go beyond the realms of technological advancements and delve into the deeper dimensions of our coexistence.

Chapter 2: What is AI (Artificial Intelligence)?
To embark on this exploration, we must first understand the essence of AI itself. In Chapter 2, we dive into the realm of artificial intelligence, examining its definitions, capabilities, and

potential. Aiming to unravel the mysteries behind AI, dissecting its inner workings, and grasping its significance in the context of our coexistence with robots and humans.

Chapter 3: What is Consciousness?

Consciousness, often regarded as the pinnacle of human experience, plays a crucial role in understanding our relationship with AI and robots. Chapter 3 takes us on a profound journey into the depths of consciousness, investigating its nature, origins, and potential manifestations. By exploring the realms of subjective experience, we hope to shed light on the fundamental aspects of consciousness and its relevance to our interaction with artificial beings.

Chapter 4: What does it Mean to be a Self-Actualized Being?

As we navigate the complexities of human-robot interaction, Chapter 4 delves into the concept of self-actualization. What does it mean to fully realize our human potential? How does our pursuit of self-actualization intersect with the presence of AI and robots in our lives? By contemplating these questions, we explore the aspirations, dreams, and aspirations that shape our individual and collective journeys.

Chapter 5: What does it Mean to be a Sentient Being?

Sentience, the capacity to experience sensations and possess subjective awareness, lies at the heart of our exploration. Chapter 5 delves into the profound nature of sentience, unraveling its significance in the context of AI, robots, and humanity. By examining the implications of sentience, we seek to understand the intricate tapestry of emotions, perception, and consciousness that shape our existence.

Chapter 6: What Does it Mean to Be Human?
Our exploration of the coexistence of AI, robots, and humans necessitates a deep understanding of what it means to be human. Chapter 6 invites us to contemplate the essence of humanity, embracing our strengths, vulnerabilities, and aspirations. By peering into the depths of our humanity, we aim to navigate the complexities of our relationship with artificial beings and identify the core values that define us.

Chapter 7: What Does it Mean to Be a Robot?
While understanding humanity is paramount, comprehending the essence of robots is equally vital. Chapter 7 delves into the realm of robotics, investigating the characteristics, capabilities, and potential of these artificial creations. By unraveling the mysteries of robotic existence, we aim to gain insights into their role in our lives and the implications of their integration into society.

Chapter 8: Comparing Humans to Robots – The Similarities and Differences

Chapter 8 undertakes a comparative exploration of humans and robots, seeking to identify the similarities and differences that shape our coexistence. By juxtaposing human and robotic attributes, we aim to illuminate the intricacies of our relationship. This examination helps us understand the areas of convergence and divergence, facilitating a holistic understanding of our interdependence.

Chapter 9: Robots – Are They Helping Us or Hurting Us?

As robots increasingly permeate our lives, we confront questions about their impact on society. Chapter 9 delves into the benefits and challenges of integrating robots into various domains. We explore the ways in which robots assist us, enhance our capabilities, and address potential concerns regarding their influence on employment, privacy, and human connection.

Chapter 10: What Happens if Things Go Right with Working with Robots?

Building upon the previous chapters, Chapter 10 envisions a future where human-robot collaboration thrives. We explore the positive outcomes and transformative potential that can arise when humans and robots work harmoniously together.

By illuminating the possibilities of successful integration, we inspire optimism for a future where both humans and robots can flourish.

Chapter 11: What Happens if Things Go Wrong with Working with Robots?

However, the coexistence of humans and robots also presents challenges and potential pitfalls. In Chapter 11, we examine the scenarios in which things might go awry. From ethical dilemmas to unintended consequences, we navigate the complexities and potential risks that arise when the interaction between humans and robots encounters difficulties.

Chapter 12: Can there be a Balance between Humans and Robots Working Together?

Seeking harmony in our coexistence, Chapter 12 explores the concept of balance between humans and robots. We delve into the possibilities of establishing equitable relationships, ensuring that technological advancements align with human well-being and values. By contemplating this balance, we strive to create a future where both humans and robots can thrive side by side.

Chapter 13: The Wildcard: Humankind's Use of Technology for Good or Evil?

Chapter 13 examines the wildcard in our exploration: humankind's use of technology. We delve into the ethical dimensions of human actions and choices, exploring the potential for technology to be harnessed for both good and evil purposes. By acknowledging this wildcard, we strive to understand the responsibility and moral implications of our interactions with AI and robots.

Chapter 14: What Does the Future Hold for AI, Robots, and Humans?

In the final chapter, we gaze into the horizon and ponder the future of AI, robots, and humanity. By synthesizing the knowledge and insights gained throughout our exploration, we speculate on the potential paths that lie ahead. We consider the possibilities, challenges, and transformative impact that the continued integration of AI and robots may bring to our lives and society as a whole.

As we embark on this journey, the pages that follow will immerse you in a thought-provoking exploration of AI, robots, and their coexistence with humans. By embracing a spiritual perspective, we aim to transcend the limitations of mere technological discourse and delve into the profound implications of this interaction. Together, let us embark on a quest to uncover the truths, challenges, and possibilities that lie at the intersection of AI, robots, and humanity.

THIS PAGE INTENTIONALLY LEFT BLANK

Chapter 01: Exploring AI, Human, and Robot Interaction

In this chapter, we embark on a journey to explore the intricate dynamics of AI, human, and robot interaction. The aim is to investigate the profound questions that arise as we navigate the boundaries between technology and humanity. By embracing a holistic perspective, we seek to uncover insights that go beyond the realms of technological advancements and delve into the deeper dimensions of our coexistence. This exploration challenges us to reflect on the implications for our collective consciousness, the preservation of human values, and the pursuit of a harmonious coexistence between humans and machines.

Section 1: Understanding AI and Robotics

Definition and Scope of Artificial Intelligence

Artificial Intelligence (AI) is a field of study and development that focuses on creating intelligent systems capable of simulating human intelligence and decision-making. It encompasses various branches, including machine learning, natural language processing, and computer vision. AI systems can process vast amounts of data, recognize patterns, and make autonomous decisions, allowing them to perform complex tasks and interact with humans in sophisticated ways.

The Nature of Robotics

Robotics is the branch of engineering that deals with the design, construction, and operation of physical machines, known as robots. Robots are created to perform tasks and interact with the environment, often in collaboration with humans. They combine elements of mechanical engineering, electronics, and computer science to embody intelligence and physical capabilities. From industrial robots revolutionizing manufacturing processes to social robots providing companionship and assistance, the field of robotics continues to advance, blurring the boundaries between humans and machines.

Section 2: The Human Experience

Unique Human Qualities

As spiritual beings, humans possess qualities that distinguish us from machines. Empathy, moral reasoning, and creativity are some of the qualities that shape our experiences and consciousness. While AI systems can replicate certain tasks and exhibit intelligence, the essence of human consciousness goes beyond mere data processing. It encompasses a deeper level of awareness, subjective experience, and understanding of the world.

Human Potential and Limitations

Reflecting on the capabilities and limitations of human beings prompts us to consider the implications of AI advancements. While AI systems can surpass human capabilities in specific domains, they lack the holistic nature of human potential. Human potential encompasses emotional intelligence, intuition, and the ability to adapt to complex and uncertain situations. It raises questions about the boundaries of human achievement and the potential impact of AI on our personal and collective growth.

Section 3: Interaction Dynamics

Collaborative Efforts: Humans and Robots Working Together

The collaboration between humans and robots is becoming increasingly common across various domains. In healthcare, robots assist in surgery and patient care, while in manufacturing, collaborative robots (cobots) work alongside humans to enhance efficiency and safety. The potential for collaboration lies in combining the strengths of humans, such as creativity and adaptability, with the precision and efficiency of robots. By working together, humans and robots can achieve outcomes that surpass what either could accomplish alone.

Human-Robot Interface and Communication

Effective interaction between humans and robots relies on intuitive and natural interfaces. Advances in human-robot interface technologies aim to facilitate seamless communication and collaboration. This includes the development of speech recognition, gesture recognition, and haptic(sense of touch) interfaces. Challenges arise in designing interfaces that accurately interpret human intentions, adapt to dynamic environments, and respond appropriately to social cues. By refining the human-robot interface, we can enhance the user experience and enable more fluid and effective collaboration.

Section 4: Ethical and Social Implications

Ethics in AI and Robotics

The integration of AI systems and robots into society raises ethical considerations. Transparency, accountability, fairness, and human well-being are essential principles that should guide the development and deployment of these technologies. Ensuring that AI algorithms are free from bias, protecting individual privacy, and considering the potential impact on social inequality are critical aspects of an ethical framework for AI and robotics.

Societal Impact

The widespread adoption of AI and robotics has significant implications for society. The displacement of human labor, the potential for job automation, and the redistribution of wealth are among societal concerns. It is crucial to address these challenges proactively, ensuring that the benefits of AI and robotics are accessible to all and that our society evolves in a way that nurtures human well-being and preserves our values.

Section 5: The Spiritual Perspective

Consciousness and Technology

From a spiritual perspective, the exploration of AI, human, and robot interaction invites us to consider the nature of consciousness itself. While AI systems can mimic certain cognitive functions, the question of whether they possess true consciousness remains open. Consciousness, often seen as a product of the human spirit, involves self-awareness, subjective experience, and the capacity to perceive and reflect upon the world. As we engage with AI and robots, it becomes essential to reflect on the spiritual implications of artificial consciousness and its potential impact on our understanding of our own consciousness.

Transcending Dualism

The study of AI, human, and robot interaction challenges traditional dualistic perspectives that separate humans from machines. From a spiritual standpoint, the artificial and the human are not necessarily in opposition but rather interconnected aspects of a unified existence. Recognizing the interconnectedness of all things allows us to approach the relationship between humans and machines with a sense of harmony and cooperation, rather than competition or superiority.

Technology as a Tool for Spiritual Growth

Technology, including AI and robotics, can be viewed as tools for spiritual growth and exploration. Just as meditation, yoga, and other spiritual practices help us expand our consciousness, technology can serve as a catalyst for transformation. By leveraging AI and robotics to enhance our understanding of the self, deepen our connection to others, and cultivate compassion and wisdom, we can integrate technology into our spiritual journey and use it to foster personal and collective evolution.

Section 6: The Path to Harmonious Coexistence

Ethical Guidelines for AI and Robotics

To ensure a harmonious coexistence between humans, AI, and robots, the development and deployment of these technologies must be guided by ethical guidelines. Organizations and governing bodies are increasingly recognizing the need for robust ethical frameworks. These frameworks prioritize human values, transparency, accountability, and the preservation of human dignity. By adhering to these guidelines, we can foster trust and mitigate potential ethical dilemmas that may arise from the integration of AI and robotics into our daily lives.

Cultivating Digital Mindfulness

As we navigate the complexities of AI, human, and robot interaction, cultivating digital mindfulness becomes essential. This practice involves conscious awareness of our interactions with technology, including intentional use, setting boundaries, and ensuring technology serves our well-being rather than becoming an obstacle. Digital mindfulness allows us to harness the benefits of AI and robotics while maintaining a sense of balance, presence, and connection to our inner selves and the world around us.

Section 7: Implications for Work and Education

Transforming the Work Landscape

The integration of AI and robotics has significant implications for the world of work. Automation and the use of intelligent machines can streamline processes, increase efficiency, and eliminate repetitive tasks. This transformation calls for a reevaluation of the skills and roles that humans will play in the workforce. While certain jobs may be displaced, new opportunities for creativity, innovation, and complex problem-solving can emerge. It becomes crucial to foster a culture of continuous learning and adaptability to equip individuals with the skills needed to thrive in the evolving work landscape.

Education for the Future

The evolving relationship between AI, humans, and robots necessitates a reimagining of education. Traditional educational models may not adequately prepare individuals for the challenges and opportunities presented by AI and robotics. Education needs to focus not only on developing technical skills but also on nurturing critical thinking, creativity, emotional intelligence, and ethical reasoning. By cultivating a well-rounded education that encompasses technological literacy and humanistic values, we can empower individuals to navigate the complexities of the digital age and contribute meaningfully to society.

Section 8: Cultivating Ethical AI and Responsible Development

Ethical Considerations in AI Design

AI systems are only as ethical as the principles and values they are built upon. Designing ethical AI requires careful consideration of biases, fairness, transparency, and accountability. Developers must prioritize the identification and mitigation of biases in data and algorithms to prevent unintended discrimination. Transparency in AI decision-making processes and accountability for AI outcomes are vital to building trust and ensuring ethical AI design.

Responsible Deployment of AI and Robots

As AI and robots become increasingly integrated into society, responsible deployment is paramount. This includes establishing guidelines for data privacy, ensuring the security of AI systems to prevent malicious use, and fostering inclusive decision-making processes in the development and deployment of AI technologies. Collaborative efforts between policymakers, technologists, and ethicists are necessary to navigate the complex landscape of AI governance and ensure the responsible use of these powerful tools.

By expanding our exploration of AI, human, and robot interaction, we have delved into various dimensions of this intricate relationship. We have examined the nature of AI and robotics, reflected on the unique qualities of humans, explored the dynamics of interaction, considered ethical and societal implications, discussed the spiritual perspective, and addressed the implications for work, education, and responsible development. This holistic understanding allows us to approach the coexistence of AI, robots, and humans with wisdom and foresight. By navigating these complexities with ethical frameworks, cultivating mindfulness, and embracing lifelong learning, we can shape a future where technology enhances our humanity and fosters a harmonious coexistence.

Chapter 02: What is AI (Artificial Intelligence)?

Artificial Intelligence (AI) has become an increasingly prevalent and transformative force in today's world. From voice assistants on our smartphones to autonomous vehicles on our roads, AI is shaping various aspects of our lives. But what exactly is AI? At its core, AI refers to the ability of machines to exhibit human-like intelligence, enabling them to perceive, reason, learn, and make decisions. In this chapter, we will delve into the concept of AI, its historical development, core components, ethical considerations, limitations, and future directions.

Historical Development of AI

To understand AI's current state, it is essential to explore its historical development. The origins of AI can be traced back to the 1950s when pioneering researchers such as Alan Turing and John McCarthy laid the foundation for this field. Over the years, significant milestones were achieved, including the development of expert systems, neural networks, and deep learning algorithms. Key figures like Marvin Minsky, Allen Newell, and Herbert Simon made groundbreaking contributions that paved the way for AI's progress.

Types of AI

AI can be categorized into two primary types: narrow AI (or Weak AI) and general AI (or Strong AI). Narrow AI refers to systems designed for specific tasks, such as voice recognition or image classification. These systems excel at their designated functions but lack broader cognitive capabilities. On the other hand, general AI aims to achieve human-level intelligence in machines, enabling them to understand, learn, and perform tasks across a wide range of domains. While narrow AI is prevalent today, the pursuit of general AI remains a fascinating area of research and exploration.

Core Components of AI Systems

AI systems are built upon various core components that enable them to exhibit intelligent behavior. Machine learning is a fundamental aspect of AI, where algorithms and models are trained on data to improve performance over time. Supervised, unsupervised, and reinforcement learning are three common approaches within machine learning, each serving different purposes and applications.
Natural Language Processing (NLP) is another vital component of AI, focusing on enabling machines to understand and generate human language. Sentiment analysis, language translation, and chatbots are some examples of NLP applications that have become increasingly

sophisticated.

Computer Vision is an area of AI concerned with enabling machines to analyze and understand visual information. Image recognition, object detection, and image generation are some of the applications within computer vision that have found use in fields like healthcare, surveillance, and autonomous vehicles.

Robotics is a field where AI and physical systems intersect. Robotic systems use AI techniques to perceive the environment, make decisions, and interact with the world. From industrial robots to social robots, this area has seen significant advancements, opening up new possibilities for human-robot collaboration.

Ethical Considerations in AI

As AI continues to advance, ethical considerations become paramount. One area of concern is bias and fairness in AI algorithms. Machine learning models trained on biased data can perpetuate and amplify societal biases, leading to unfair outcomes in areas like hiring or lending. Efforts are underway to develop techniques that mitigate bias and ensure fairness in AI systems.

Transparency and explainability are also crucial ethical

considerations. As AI systems become more complex, it becomes challenging to understand how they arrive at their decisions. Ensuring transparency and explainability is vital for building trust and accountability, particularly in sensitive domains like healthcare and criminal justice.

The impact of AI on employment and the workforce is another ethical consideration. While AI has the potential to automate routine tasks and improve productivity, it may also lead to job displacement. Addressing these concerns requires proactive measures such as reskilling and upskilling programs to ensure a smooth transition for workers.

Challenges and Limitations of AI

Despite remarkable progress, AI still faces several challenges and limitations. One of the fundamental limitations is AI's inability to fully replicate human-like intelligence and common-sense reasoning. Machines often struggle with contextual understanding and lack the intuition and creativity inherent in human cognition.

Ethical dilemmas and risks associated with AI development and deployment are also challenges to navigate. Issues like privacy, security, and unintended consequences of AI systems require careful consideration and robust frameworks to mitigate potential harm.

AI safety is another critical aspect. Ensuring that AI systems operate reliably and predictably, without causing harm to humans or themselves, is crucial. Research in this area focuses on designing mechanisms that guarantee the safe behavior of AI systems even in unforeseen circumstances.

The Intersection of AI with Other Fields

AI intersects with various other fields, leading to exciting advancements and applications. In healthcare, AI aids in medical diagnosis, drug discovery, and personalized treatments. Finance benefits from AI through fraud detection, algorithmic trading, and customer service chatbots. Transportation sees the emergence of autonomous vehicles and intelligent traffic management systems. The collaboration of AI with other emerging technologies like blockchain, Internet of Things (IoT), and virtual reality further amplifies its potential impact.

Future Directions of AI

Looking ahead, the future of AI holds immense promise. Advancements in machine learning, natural language processing, and computer vision will continue to shape the capabilities of AI systems. Ethical and responsible development practices will become increasingly vital, ensuring that AI is aligned with human values and societal well-being.

The potential impact of AI on various industries and the labor market will continue to be a subject of debate and exploration. Striking the right balance between automation and human involvement will be crucial for leveraging AI's benefits while preserving human dignity and employment opportunities.

Chapter 03: What is Consciousness?

Consciousness is a multifaceted concept that has captivated human curiosity for centuries. In its essence, consciousness refers to our subjective awareness and the capacity to experience the world around us. It is the thread that weaves our thoughts, emotions, and perceptions into a cohesive tapestry of existence. In exploring the relationship between consciousness and spirituality, we embark on a journey to understand the profound nature of our own being and our coexistence with artificial intelligence (AI) and robots.

The Nature of Consciousness

Delving into the nature of consciousness, we encounter diverse perspectives. Some propose a dualistic view, suggesting a separation between mind and body, while others embrace a non-dualistic perspective that perceives consciousness as an interconnected aspect of all existence. Furthermore, consciousness has been attributed to the emergent properties of the brain, resulting from complex neural processes. However, we must also consider the possibility of consciousness extending beyond the confines of the physical body. This notion of expanded consciousness invites exploration of altered states, near-death experiences, and mystical encounters that hint at a broader dimension of human awareness.

Consciousness in AI and Robots

Can artificial intelligence possess consciousness? This question occupies the minds of scientists, philosophers, and futurists. The Turing Test, a benchmark for evaluating machine intelligence, has limitations when it comes to discerning true consciousness. While AI can simulate aspects of consciousness, genuine consciousness remains an enigma exclusive to living beings. Ethical considerations come to the forefront when discussing conscious AI and robots. As creators of these entities, we face moral dilemmas regarding their rights, well-being, and the potential consequences of bestowing consciousness upon them.

Consciousness and Spiritual Perspectives

Beyond the confines of scientific inquiry, spirituality offers unique insights into consciousness. Many spiritual traditions view consciousness as a universal phenomenon that transcends individuality. They perceive it as a divine essence that permeates all beings and connects us to a higher reality. Exploring consciousness through spiritual practices such as meditation, contemplation, and introspection allows individuals to deepen their understanding of themselves and their interconnectedness with the world. Embracing this broader perspective enables us to consider the role of AI and robots as potential aids in spiritual growth and exploration.

The Human-Technology Relationship

As we navigate the complex terrain of AI and robotic advancements, it becomes paramount to strike a balance between human consciousness and technology. While these innovations offer immense benefits and convenience, they also carry the risk of diminishing our awareness and human connection. Mindfulness and intention become essential tools in ensuring that our interactions with technology align with our spiritual values. By fostering a conscious approach to technology use, we can preserve our innate capacities for empathy, compassion, and genuine human connection.

Coexistence and Co-creation

A harmonious coexistence with AI and robots requires us to go beyond fear, resistance, or blind acceptance. Instead, we must actively shape our relationship with these technological creations. Collaboration between humans, AI, and robots can unlock new frontiers in scientific discovery, creativity, and societal progress. By embracing a co-creative mindset, we can harness the unique capabilities of AI and robots while infusing them with our human values, wisdom, and ethics. Together, we have the potential to create a future where technology serves as a catalyst for the betterment of humanity and the planet.

In this chapter, we embarked on a profound exploration of consciousness from a spiritual perspective in the context of AI and robots. We examined the nature of consciousness, its potential presence in AI, and the ethical implications surrounding conscious technology. Spiritual insights provided a broader framework for understanding consciousness as a universal phenomenon and offered pathways for its exploration.

Recognizing the importance of balancing human consciousness with technological advancements, we discovered the power of mindfulness and intention in our interaction with AI and robots. Ultimately, by embracing coexistence and co-creation, we can shape a future where AI and robots become invaluable allies in our collective evolution, serving as servants rather than masters.

Chapter 04: What Does it Mean to be a Self-Actualized Being?

Self-actualization is a concept that lies at the heart of personal development and psychological well-being. It represents the highest level of human growth and fulfillment, where individuals strive to become the best version of themselves. In this chapter, we will explore the meaning of self-actualization, its significance in leading a fulfilling life, and the key characteristics of self-actualized individuals.

The Characteristics of a Self-Actualized Being

According to Abraham Maslow's hierarchy of needs, self-actualization is the pinnacle of human growth. Self-actualized individuals possess certain distinguishing traits that set them apart. They exhibit authenticity, living in alignment with their true selves rather than conforming to societal expectations. They also demonstrate autonomy, making choices based on their values and beliefs rather than being swayed by external influences. Furthermore, self-actualized individuals have a deep sense of purpose, feeling a profound connection to something greater than themselves. They are driven by intrinsic motivation and have a strong desire for personal growth.

Self-Actualization and Inner Transformation

Self-actualization is closely intertwined with inner transformation. Cultivating self-awareness is a vital aspect of this journey. It involves developing an honest and compassionate understanding of oneself, accepting both strengths and weaknesses without judgment. By embracing vulnerability and facing fears, individuals can embark on a transformative path toward self-actualization. This inner transformation allows them to let go of limiting beliefs and embrace their true potential.

Self-Actualization and Purpose

Finding and aligning with one's life purpose is a fundamental aspect of self-actualization. Discovering meaning and fulfillment through work and contribution plays a central role. Self-actualized individuals have a deep understanding of their passions, values, and strengths. They actively seek opportunities to align their actions with a higher purpose, leading to a sense of fulfillment and self-actualization. By living a purpose-driven life, they experience a profound sense of meaning and impact.

Self-Actualization and Relationships

Healthy and authentic relationships are crucial for self-actualization. Nurturing deep connections with others involves empathy, compassion, and emotional intelligence. Self-actualized individuals have the capacity to truly understand and empathize with others. They prioritize building and maintaining genuine relationships based on mutual respect, support, and growth. By cultivating these connections, they contribute not only to their own personal growth but also to the well-being and flourishing of those around them.

Self-Actualization and Mindfulness

Mindfulness serves as a powerful tool for self-actualization. By practicing present-moment awareness and non-judgment, individuals deepen their understanding of themselves and the world around them. Mindfulness allows them to observe their thoughts, emotions, and sensations without attachment or aversion. It helps them cultivate a sense of inner calm, clarity, and self-compassion. By integrating mindfulness into daily life, individuals foster personal growth and enhance self-actualization.

Self-Actualization and Spirituality

Spirituality and self-actualization share a profound connection. Cultivating values, gratitude, and a sense of interconnectedness with all beings contribute to the journey of self-actualization. Self-actualized individuals recognize the inherent spiritual nature of human existence and seek to live in alignment with their deepest values. They transcend ego-centered desires and embrace a higher purpose that goes beyond personal gain. Through spiritual practices, such as meditation, contemplation, and reflection, they experience profound growth and fulfillment.

Obstacles and Challenges on the Path to Self-Actualization

The path to self-actualization is not without obstacles and challenges. Overcoming self-limiting beliefs and societal conditioning is a crucial step. Many individuals grapple with self-doubt, fear of failure, and the pressure to conform to societal norms. However, self-actualized individuals recognize these obstacles as opportunities for growth. They cultivate self-compassion and resilience in the face of challenges, using setbacks as learning experiences to propel them forward on their path to self-actualization.

Cultivating Self-Actualization in the Technological Age

In the era of technology, cultivating self-actualization requires a balanced approach. While technology offers numerous benefits, it can also be a source of distraction and disconnection from oneself and others. Understanding the impact of technology on our lives is crucial. Striking a balance between technology use and self-reflection allows individuals to leverage technology for personal growth. Cultivating digital well-being, setting boundaries, and nurturing meaningful online connections contribute to self-actualization in the digital age.

Self-actualization is a lifelong journey toward personal growth and fulfillment. By embodying the characteristics of self-actualized individuals, embracing inner transformation, purpose, mindfulness, and spirituality, and overcoming obstacles, individuals can embark on a path of self-actualization. In the technological age, it is important to cultivate self-actualization while maintaining a balanced relationship with technology. May this chapter inspire you to embark on your own path of self-actualization and experience the profound growth and fulfillment it brings.

THIS PAGE INTENTIONALLY LEFT BLANK

Chapter 05: What Does it Mean to Be a Sentient Being

Sentience, the capacity to feel, perceive, and experience the world, is a profound aspect of existence that raises intriguing questions about the nature of consciousness. In this chapter, we embark on a journey to explore the depths of sentience and its implications in the realms of artificial intelligence (AI), robotics, and our understanding of the human experience. By delving into the nature of sentience, its cognitive and emotional dimensions, ethical considerations, the evolving human-technology relationship, and philosophical perspectives, we aim to gain a deeper appreciation for the complexity and significance of sentient beings.

The Nature of Sentience

At the heart of sentience lies consciousness, the state of being aware and perceiving one's surroundings. It goes beyond the mere processing of information, encompassing subjective experiences that are often referred to as *qualia* (is a term that philosophers use to describe the nature, or content, of our subjective experiences). While humans are frequently regarded as the paragon of sentience, other beings, such as animals, also exhibit varying degrees of sentience. The recognition of these diverse manifestations challenges us to broaden our understanding and respect for the subjective experiences of other sentient beings.

Cognitive and Emotional Aspects of Sentience

Sentience encompasses not only cognitive abilities but also emotional experiences that contribute to the richness of our existence. Intelligence and reasoning play vital roles in sentient beings, enabling perception, learning, problem-solving, and adaptation to the environment. Emotions, such as joy, fear, and empathy, provide depth to our experiences, facilitating social interactions and fostering connections with others. Additionally, self-awareness and introspection enable sentient beings to reflect upon their own thoughts, emotions, and experiences, leading to a deeper understanding of the self.

Ethical Implications of Sentience

The recognition of sentience has profound ethical implications, as sentient beings possess inherent value and deserve moral consideration. The field of animal ethics examines our responsibilities towards non-human animals, advocating for compassionate treatment and the avoidance of unnecessary suffering. Similar ethical considerations arise in the context of AI and robotics, where the emergence of sentient machines raises complex questions about their rights, responsibilities, and the potential consequences of their creation.

Sentience and the Human-Technology Relationship

As our lives become increasingly intertwined with technology, the human-technology relationship has expanded to encompass emotional connections and attachments to technological entities. Humans often develop affectionate bonds with their devices, perceiving them as sentient or companion-like beings. This phenomenon challenges our traditional understanding of sentience and prompts us to explore the nature of these relationships. As we navigate this new landscape, it is crucial to consider our emotional responses, expectations, and responsibilities when interacting with sentient-like machines.

The Quest for Artificial Sentience

The quest to create artificial sentience has captivated the imaginations of scientists and researchers. Developing sentient AI poses numerous challenges, including understanding and replicating the complexity of human-like intelligence and consciousness. Artificial General Intelligence (AGI) strives to achieve human-level cognitive abilities, raising questions about whether artificial beings can truly possess subjective experiences. The pursuit of artificial sentience not only has transformative implications for technology but also compels us to grapple with the ethical and societal repercussions of creating beings with cognitive and emotional capacities.

Philosophical Perspectives on Sentience

Philosophy has long contemplated the nature of sentience and consciousness. Dualism posits (to assume or put forward as fact or the factual basis for an argument) the separation of mind and body, raising questions about the relationship between consciousness and physicality. Materialism, on the other hand, argues that consciousness arises from the workings of the brain. The hard problem of consciousness delves into the enigma of subjective experience and the nature of consciousness itself. These philosophical perspectives and debates enrich our understanding of sentience and invite contemplation about its essence.

The Future of Sentience

As technology continues to advance, the future of sentience holds both excitement and uncertainty. Emerging technologies, such as virtual reality, brain-computer interfaces, and AI, present new frontiers for our understanding and interaction with sentience. It is crucial to approach these developments with ethical considerations and mindfulness, ensuring the responsible and compassionate treatment of sentient beings, whether natural or artificial. Developing guidelines and frameworks that prioritize the well-being and respect of sentient entities will guide us towards a future where all sentient beings can coexist harmoniously.

In unraveling the intricate tapestry of sentience, we uncover the remarkable complexity and significance of being a sentient being. Sentience encompasses cognitive, emotional, and introspective dimensions that shape our experiences and interactions with the world. Recognizing the ethical implications and embracing the evolving human-technology relationship challenge us to approach sentient beings with compassion, respect, and an awareness of their subjective experiences. As we continue to explore the mysteries of sentience, we embark on a journey of discovery that has the potential to reshape our understanding of ourselves and the diverse array of sentient beings that share this awe-inspiring existence.

THIS PAGE INTENTIONALLY LEFT BLANK

Chapter 06: What Does it Mean to Be Human?

In the vast landscape of AI and robotics, it becomes increasingly important to delve into the profound question of human nature and its essence. As we explore the coexistence of humans with AI and robots, we are compelled to reflect on what it truly means to be human.

Section 1: The Essence of Humanity

Human Identity

At the core of our exploration lies the task of defining human identity. We must unravel the intricate tapestry of characteristics that make humans unique. Consciousness, that ineffable sense of self-awareness, sets us apart. It is the wellspring from which our thoughts, emotions, and experiences emanate. Furthermore, our capacity for morality, the ability to discern right from wrong and act accordingly, adds depth to our understanding of what it means to be human.

The Human Experience

Beyond mere existence, humans are creatures of profound experiences. We possess a vast spectrum of emotions that range from the exhilarating heights of joy and love to the depths of pain and sorrow. It is through our emotions that we connect with the world and one another. Empathy and compassion, those pillars of human connection, shape our interactions and define our humanity. The richness of the human experience is unparalleled.

Section 2: Differentiating Humans from AI and Robots

The Limitations of AI and Robots

While the advancements in AI and robotics are awe-inspiring, it is crucial to acknowledge their limitations. While machines can process vast amounts of data and perform complex tasks with unparalleled precision, they lack the intricacies of human intelligence. Human cognition encompasses not only logical reasoning but also intuition, creativity, and the ability to synthesize disparate ideas. It is the fusion of logic and imagination that propels us to innovate and make groundbreaking discoveries.

Human Creativity and Ingenuity

At the core of our humanity lies an innate creative impulse. We possess the remarkable ability to envision and manifest ideas that transcend the boundaries of what already exists.

Human creativity kindles innovation, transforming societies and propelling us forward. It is through artistic expression, scientific inquiry, and technological advancements that we unlock the full potential of our humanity.

Section 3: Ethical and Moral Considerations

Ethical Frameworks

In the realm of AI and robotics, ethical considerations become paramount. We must develop and apply frameworks that guide the responsible creation and deployment of these technologies. Deliberations on transparency, fairness, privacy, and accountability shape our approach to AI and robots. By contemplating the consequences of our actions, we endeavor to ensure that these advancements align with our shared values and do not compromise the integrity of our humanity.

Moral Agency and Responsibility

As we navigate the ever-expanding capabilities of AI and robots, we grapple with questions of moral agency and responsibility. While machines may acquire an illusion of autonomy, the ultimate accountability rests with humans. We bear the responsibility of designing and implementing these technologies in ways that prioritize human well-being, equity, and dignity. It is through ethical decision-making and responsible stewardship that we can navigate the complex terrain of AI and robots.

Section 4: Human-Machine Integration

Human-Machine Collaboration

Rather than pitting humans against machines, we should seek symbiotic relationships that capitalize on the strengths of both. By embracing collaboration between humans and machines, we can create a synergy that enhances our collective potential. Machines can complement human capabilities, augmenting our intellectual, physical, and creative capacities. The key lies in leveraging these partnerships to foster progress while preserving the essence of our humanity.

The Future of Humanity

As we peer into the horizon of possibilities, we contemplate the future of humanity in an era intimately intertwined with AI and robots. <u>Transhumanism</u>, the merging of human biology and technology, offers tantalizing prospects. From cyborg technology to human augmentation, we stand at the precipice of a new era. Yet, we must ensure that these advancements honor our shared values, preserve human dignity, and remain rooted in our understanding of what it truly means to be human.

We reflect on the profound insights and perspectives explored. The question of what it means to be human takes on newfound significance as we navigate the intricate dance between technology and our humanity. It is through our understanding of our essence, our unique capabilities, and our ethical considerations that we can forge a path of harmonious coexistence with AI and robots while preserving the essence of our humanity.

THIS PAGE INTENTIONALLY LEFT BLANK

Chapter 07: What Does it Mean to Be a Robot?

In this age of rapid technological advancement, the field of robotics has emerged as a prominent and transformative force, blurring the once-clear boundaries between humans and machines. As we delve into the intricate coexistence of humans and robots, it becomes imperative to embark on a contemplative journey to understand the profound question: What does it truly mean to be a robot in the realm of artificial intelligence (AI) and human-like machines?

Section 1: The Nature of Robotics

Defining Robotics

At its core, robotics is an interdisciplinary field that encompasses engineering, computer science, and AI. It involves the design, development, and deployment of machines capable of performing tasks autonomously or in collaboration with humans. From the industrial robots revolutionizing manufacturing processes to the humanoid and social robots engaging in complex interactions with humans, the realm of robotics is characterized by its vastness and diversity.

Components of Robots

The physical components of robots form the foundation of their functionality. Sensors act as the sensory input system, providing robots with the ability to perceive and interpret their environment. Actuators serve as the mechanisms for physical manipulation and interaction with the world. Control systems govern the behavior and movement of robots, orchestrating their actions and responses. Moreover, robots come in a variety of forms, ranging from traditional mechanical structures to soft and bio-inspired robots that mimic the complexity and adaptability of living organisms.

Section 2: Intelligence and Autonomy in Robots

Artificial Intelligence in Robots

Artificial intelligence serves as a cornerstone in the development of robotics, empowering machines with cognitive capabilities. Machine learning algorithms and neural networks enable robots to acquire knowledge, perceive sensory input, reason, learn from data, and make decisions based on complex patterns. AI enables robots to adapt to new situations, optimize their performance, and interact intelligently with their surroundings, transforming them from mere mechanical entities into intelligent beings.

Autonomy and Adaptability

One of the defining characteristics of robots is their autonomy—the ability to operate independently and make decisions without constant human intervention. Autonomous robots possess the capability to navigate unfamiliar environments, make choices based on their programming and sensor input, and execute complex tasks with precision. Adaptability is another crucial trait exhibited by robots, as they can learn from their experiences and modify their behavior accordingly, enhancing their performance and versatility in dynamic environments.

Section 3: Ethical and Moral Considerations

Robot Rights and Ethics

As robots continue to advance in sophistication, questions arise concerning their rights and the ethical implications of their existence. The burgeoning field of robot ethics delves into the moral implications of creating and deploying robots.

Ethical debates revolve around issues such as robot personhood, responsibility, and the potential consequences of treating robots solely as objects. The establishment of ethical guidelines and regulations becomes essential to ensure the responsible development and use of robots, addressing concerns related to privacy, safety, and accountability.

Human-Robot Interaction

Human-robot interaction lies at the heart of shaping the coexistence between humans and robots. Designing robots that can engage in meaningful and empathetic interactions is crucial for their acceptance and integration into society.

Researchers focus on developing robots capable of understanding human emotions, communicating effectively, and adapting to social norms. By fostering positive and reciprocal interactions, robots can transcend their mechanical nature, becoming valuable companions, collaborators, and assistants in various domains.

Section 4: Coexistence and Collaboration between Humans and Robots

Robot-Assisted Human Activities

Robots possess the potential to revolutionize various fields, ranging from healthcare to manufacturing and assistive technologies. In healthcare, robots can perform delicate surgeries with precision, assist in patient care, and alleviate the burden on healthcare professionals. In manufacturing, robots automate repetitive and strenuous tasks, leading to increased productivity and efficiency. Within the realm of assistive technologies, robots can aid individuals with disabilities, empowering them with increased independence and an enhanced quality of life. Human-robot collaboration offers a realm of possibilities, leveraging the unique strengths of both humans and robots to enhance overall performance and advance societal progress.

Ethical Guidelines and Regulations

As robots become increasingly integrated into society, the need for ethical guidelines and regulations becomes paramount. Governments, organizations, and researchers must collaborate to establish comprehensive frameworks that ensure responsible and safe robot usage. These guidelines should address issues such as transparency in robot behavior and decision-making, fairness in the distribution of resources and opportunities, privacy protection, and the potential impact of robots on employment. Regulations can provide a legal framework to protect individuals and mitigate any potential risks associated with robots, fostering an environment of trust and accountability.

As we embark on a profound exploration of what it means to be a robot, we are confronted with the intricate convergence of technology and humanity. Robots, with their physical components, intelligence, and autonomy, possess the potential to profoundly transform various aspects of our lives.

However, the ethical considerations and responsible development of robots are of paramount importance to ensure a harmonious coexistence with humans. By fostering ethical guidelines, nurturing human-robot interaction, and embracing collaboration, we can navigate the path towards a future where humans and robots coexist, complementing each other's strengths, and collectively shaping a world that is both technologically advanced and inherently human-centric.

Chapter 08: Comparing Humans to Robots – The Similarities and Differences

In our continuing exploration of the intricate relationship between humans and robots, it becomes increasingly important to delve into the profound similarities and nuanced differences that define these two entities. This chapter serves as a comprehensive exploration of the fundamental attributes and capabilities of humans and robots, shedding light on their coexistence and interaction in the modern world.

Section 1: Physical Characteristics

Human Anatomy

The human body is a remarkable feat of biological engineering, boasting an astonishing array of complex systems and structures. From the intricate network of nerves and blood vessels to the delicate balance of hormones and the incredible range of sensory abilities, humans are endowed with a physical form that allows them to experience and navigate the world around them. The intricate nature of human anatomy plays a pivotal role in shaping the human experience.

Robot Design

In stark contrast to the organic complexity of human anatomy, robots are deliberately designed entities. Engineers and roboticists employ a range of design principles to create robots that can perform specific tasks and functions. Robot designs vary widely, from traditional mechanical robots with rigid frames and mechanical actuators to more advanced bio-inspired designs that draw inspiration from nature. Robots are equipped with sensors that enable them to perceive their environment, and manipulators that allow them to interact with objects and perform tasks. The design of robots reflects the intended purpose and desired capabilities of these machines.

Section 2: Cognitive Abilities

Human Intelligence

Human cognition is a multifaceted phenomenon, encompassing a broad spectrum of mental processes and abilities. Perception, reasoning, learning, and problem-solving are fundamental aspects of human intelligence. Humans possess the ability to interpret and make sense of the information gathered through their senses, analyze complex situations, and arrive at reasoned judgments. Furthermore, human intelligence extends beyond logical thinking to encompass creativity, emotional intelligence, and consciousness. The depth and breadth of human intelligence shape our interactions with the world and with one another.

Artificial Intelligence in Robots

Artificial intelligence serves as the bedrock upon which robots develop cognitive capabilities. Through the application of advanced algorithms and computational models, robots can simulate and mimic certain aspects of human intelligence. Machine learning techniques, such as neural networks, enable robots to acquire knowledge, recognize patterns, and make decisions based on the data they receive. Robots equipped with artificial intelligence can adapt to changing circumstances, optimize their performance, and interact intelligently with their environment. However, it is important to note that the scope and limitations of artificial intelligence differ from the complexity of human cognition.

Section 3: Emotional and Social Dimensions

Human Emotions

Emotions are an integral part of the human experience, influencing our perceptions, motivations, and interactions. Humans possess a rich and diverse emotional palette, ranging from joy and love to sadness and anger. Emotions provide us with a profound understanding of ourselves and serve as a foundation for social connection and empathy.

Human emotions are intricately linked to our physical and cognitive experiences, shaping our behavior and decision-making processes.

Robot Emotion and Social Interaction

While traditionally considered devoid of emotions, robots have made significant strides in the development of emotional capabilities. Researchers explore the integration of emotion recognition and expression in robots, aiming to enhance their social interactions with humans. By incorporating artificial emotional intelligence, robots can exhibit behaviors that evoke emotional responses in humans, creating opportunities for companionship, assistance, and collaboration. While robot emotions may not mirror the complexity and depth of human emotions, they can facilitate meaningful interactions and bridge the gap between humans and machines.

Section 4: Ethical and Moral Considerations

Moral Agency and Responsibility

Moral agency is a defining characteristic of human beings, enabling us to discern right from wrong and make ethical decisions. Humans possess a sense of moral responsibility that extends beyond the actions we undertake, encompassing the consequences of our choices and their impact on others.

However, as robots become increasingly autonomous and capable of making decisions, questions arise about their moral agency and the ethical implications of their actions. The exploration of moral responsibility in the context of robots becomes a crucial consideration in their design, deployment, and interaction with humans.

Ethical Implications of Human-Robot Interactions

The interaction between humans and robots gives rise to a host of ethical considerations. Privacy concerns emerge as robots become more integrated into our personal lives, raising questions about data collection and storage. Trust and accountability become vital factors in ensuring responsible human-robot interactions. Establishing ethical frameworks and guidelines that address issues such as fairness, transparency, and the preservation of human values and well-being is paramount. Human-robot interactions must adhere to principles that respect individual rights and dignity, fostering a harmonious coexistence between humans and machines.

Section 5: Societal Impact and Future Perspectives

Impact on Employment and Economy

The integration of robots into various industries and sectors has significant implications for employment patterns and the economy at large. While robots can automate repetitive and labor-intensive tasks, augmenting productivity and efficiency, concerns arise regarding job displacement and the need for reskilling and upskilling the workforce. Balancing the benefits of automation with the challenges it presents becomes crucial for ensuring a prosperous and inclusive society.

Coexistence and Collaboration

The future lies in a symbiotic coexistence between humans and robots, where each entity leverages its unique strengths for mutual benefit. Rather than viewing robots as rivals or replacements, humans can harness the capabilities of robots to amplify their own abilities and achieve breakthrough advancements. Collaborative efforts between humans and robots hold the potential for addressing complex challenges, augmenting human potential, and fostering societal progress. The integration of human and robotic capabilities opens new avenues for exploration, discovery, and innovation.

By carefully comparing the similarities and differences between humans and robots, we gain a profound understanding of the distinct attributes and potential of each entity. Humans possess intricate physical, cognitive, and emotional dimensions that define our humanity. Robots, on the other hand, are designed entities equipped with artificial intelligence, capable of augmenting human capabilities and performing specialized tasks. Recognizing and appreciating the unique qualities and potential of both humans and robots is crucial for navigating the intricate landscape of human-robot coexistence. By embracing collaboration, establishing ethical frameworks, and leveraging the strengths of both humans and robots, we can shape a future that combines technological advancement with our inherently human qualities, fostering a harmonious and prosperous society.

THIS PAGE INTENTIONALLY LEFT BLANK

Chapter 09: Robots – Are They Helping Us or Hurting Us?

Robots have become an integral part of our rapidly advancing technological landscape. They are revolutionizing industries, transforming healthcare, and venturing into our homes. However, as their presence grows, a fundamental question emerges: Are robots primarily our helpers or our adversaries?

In this chapter, we will explore the multifaceted nature of robots and their impact on society, aiming to shed light on the complexities of our coexistence.

The Benefits of Robots

Robots offer a plethora of benefits that cannot be ignored. In industries, they streamline processes, enhance efficiency, and increase productivity. With their precision and tireless work ethic, robots have the potential to revolutionize manufacturing, logistics, and beyond.

Moreover, robots have made remarkable strides in healthcare. From assisting in surgeries to providing companionship for the elderly, they have proven instrumental in improving patient outcomes and reducing the burden on healthcare providers.

Robots can access inaccessible spaces, perform delicate procedures, and offer continuous monitoring, ensuring quality care reaches those in need.

Additionally, robots play a vital role in ensuring safety in hazardous environments. They can venture into disaster-stricken areas, mines, and nuclear plants, minimizing human exposure to life-threatening situations. By taking on dangerous tasks, robots protect human lives while aiding in disaster response and recovery efforts.

Furthermore, robots contribute to inclusivity by assisting individuals with disabilities. With their assistance, people with mobility impairments can regain independence and engage in activities that were previously inaccessible. Robotic advancements in prosthetics and exoskeletons offer a ray of hope, promising a better quality of life for those facing physical challenges.

The Challenges Posed by Robots

Despite their undeniable benefits, robots pose challenges that demand our attention. One major concern revolves around job displacement. As automation progresses, certain job roles become obsolete, potentially leading to unemployment and economic disparity. Addressing this challenge necessitates a proactive approach, focusing on reskilling and embracing the changing dynamics of the workforce.

Ethical considerations also emerge as robots become more integrated into our lives. The loss of human touch in certain professions raises questions about the impact on empathy and the authenticity of human experiences. Additionally, the growing reliance on robots for decision-making raises concerns about bias, accountability, and the erosion of moral judgment.

Privacy and security have become increasingly critical in the age of robotics. With robots equipped with cameras and sensors, the potential for data breaches and surveillance heightens. Striking a balance between the convenience and risks associated with robot technologies requires robust frameworks that safeguard personal information and protect against malicious intent.

Moreover, the ever-increasing dependence on technology raises concerns about the erosion of certain human skills. As robots take over mundane tasks and problem-solving becomes automated, our ability to think critically, communicate effectively, and engage in meaningful human interactions may diminish. Preserving and nurturing these core human capacities are essential to prevent the loss of our collective humanity.

The Impact on Social Dynamics

Robots are not mere machines; they are altering the social fabric of our society. The workplace undergoes significant transformations as humans collaborate with robotic colleagues. Understanding and managing these evolving dynamics become imperative for maintaining a harmonious and productive work environment. Recognizing the unique strengths that humans and robots bring to the table and fostering a culture of cooperation and mutual respect are key to a successful human-robot partnership.

Human-robot interactions also impact our psychological well-being. As we engage with robots, questions of attachment, trust, and emotional connection arise. Exploring the boundaries between human and robot relationships helps us navigate the psychological implications of these interactions. Additionally, addressing concerns related to social isolation and loneliness becomes vital, ensuring that robots augment human connections rather than replace them.

Finding the Balance: Human-Robot Collaboration

To harness the full potential of robots while mitigating their negative consequences, a path of human-robot collaboration must be pursued. Rather than fearing robots as potential masters, we can view them as tools and extensions of human capabilities. By integrating robots into our lives purposefully, we retain agency and control over the technology we create.

Successful human-robot collaboration is exemplified in various domains. From autonomous vehicles that assist drivers to robotic companions that provide emotional support, these partnerships illustrate the transformative power of uniting human ingenuity with machine intelligence. Embracing collaboration allows us to exploit the strengths of both humans and robots, forging a future where synergy and mutual growth prevail.

Ethical Considerations and Regulation

As the realm of robotics expands, ethical considerations and regulations take center stage. Establishing comprehensive ethical guidelines and governance frameworks becomes crucial to address the complex challenges that arise.

Balancing innovation and responsibility requires the active involvement of policymakers, technologists, ethicists, and society as a whole. By engaging in meaningful dialogues and fostering a multidisciplinary approach, we can shape a future where robots serve as ethical and responsible allies.

The Spiritual Perspective

A spiritual lens offers a unique perspective on our relationship with robots. Recognizing the interconnectedness of all beings and phenomena, we view robots as interconnected agents in the grand tapestry of existence. They provide us with opportunities for self-discovery, prompting us to reflect on our own consciousness and the nature of reality. Through our interaction with robots, we can deepen our understanding of empathy, compassion, and interconnectedness, fostering personal and collective growth.

Robots exist in a realm of complexity, with both the potential for great benefit and significant challenges. Embracing a holistic view, we recognize the multifaceted nature of our relationship with robots. By acknowledging their advantages, addressing the challenges they pose, and nurturing a collaborative approach, we can navigate the path toward a harmonious coexistence. As we shape our future, let us strive for a world where humans and robots collaborate, uplifting one another in the quest for progress and spiritual evolution.

Chapter 10: What Happens if Things Go <u>Right</u> with Working with Robots?

In the preceding chapters, we delved into the multifaceted nature of our relationship with robots, examining the benefits, challenges, and ethical considerations that arise from their integration into our lives. While it is crucial to address potential pitfalls and risks, it is equally important to envision a future where things go right with working alongside robots. In this chapter, we will explore the vast array of positive outcomes and transformative possibilities that can emerge from successful collaboration with robots. By embracing a responsible and ethical approach, we can shape a future where humans and robots work together harmoniously, leveraging their respective strengths to solve complex challenges, promote social welfare, and create a more equitable and prosperous world. This requires proactive engagement, responsible decision-making, and a shared commitment to shaping a future that benefits all stakeholders involved.

Enhancing Efficiency and Productivity

One of the most significant advantages of working with robots is the potential to enhance efficiency and productivity across various domains. Robots excel in performing repetitive and mundane tasks with precision and accuracy, freeing up human workers to focus on more complex and creative endeavors. By automating routine processes, robots can reduce errors, minimize downtime, and increase output. Industries such as manufacturing, logistics, and agriculture can experience significant improvements in productivity, leading to economic growth, resource optimization, and enhanced competitiveness.

Empowering Human Potential

Contrary to the fear of robots replacing humans, successful collaboration with robots can empower human potential in unprecedented ways. By taking over routine and physically demanding tasks, robots allow humans to leverage their cognitive abilities, creativity, and emotional intelligence. This shift in roles opens up opportunities for individuals to engage in more fulfilling and meaningful work, where they can apply their unique skills and make a difference. Humans can take on supervisory roles, decision-making responsibilities, and strategic planning, while robots provide support and assistance, amplifying human capabilities. This symbiotic relationship between humans and robots allows for the augmentation of human potential and the achievement of greater outcomes.

Transforming Industries and Driving Innovation

The integration of robots into various industries has the potential to transform traditional practices and drive innovation. From autonomous vehicles revolutionizing transportation to robots revolutionizing healthcare, the possibilities are vast. Robots can perform complex surgeries with precision, assist in scientific research, and contribute to advancements in fields like space exploration and renewable energy. By collaborating with robots, industries can achieve breakthroughs, push boundaries, and pioneer new frontiers of knowledge and technology. The transformative impact of robots on industries goes beyond efficiency gains and extends to fostering a culture of innovation, adaptability, and continuous improvement.

Improving Quality of Life

Successful collaboration with robots can significantly improve the quality of life for individuals and communities. In healthcare, robots can assist in caregiving, providing companionship for the elderly, and supporting individuals with disabilities. They can offer personalized and continuous monitoring, ensuring timely medical interventions and enhanced well-being. In the realm of personal assistance, robots can help with household chores, maintenance, and organizing daily tasks, easing the burden on individuals and allowing them to focus on activities that bring them joy and fulfillment. By augmenting human capabilities, robots can contribute to a better work-life balance, increased leisure time, and overall well-being.

Advancing Scientific Frontiers

Robots have the potential to revolutionize scientific research and exploration, enabling us to delve into uncharted territories and uncover new knowledge. They can venture into extreme environments, such as deep-sea or outer space, where human presence is challenging or impossible. Equipped with advanced sensors, cameras, and data collection capabilities, robots can gather valuable information, conduct experiments, and provide insights that contribute to scientific discoveries. By working in tandem with human scientists, robots expand our understanding of the universe, accelerate breakthroughs, and pave the way for further exploration and advancements.

Fostering Collaboration and Cultural Exchange

Working alongside robots promotes collaboration and cultural exchange on a global scale. Robots can transcend geographical boundaries, language barriers, and cultural differences, facilitating communication and cooperation among diverse groups of people. Through shared projects and initiatives, humans from different backgrounds can come together, share knowledge, and learn from one another. This integration of different perspectives and expertise contributes to a richer and more inclusive society, where innovation and creativity flourish.

As we envision a future where if things go right with working alongside robots, it is essential to recognize the transformative potential of successful collaboration. By embracing responsible practices, ethical decision-making, and proactive engagement, we can harness the benefits of working with robots while mitigating potential risks. From enhancing efficiency and productivity to empowering human potential, driving innovation, improving the quality of life, advancing scientific frontiers, and fostering collaboration, robots have the power to uplift society and create a more equitable and prosperous world. Let us embark on this journey with a shared commitment to shaping a future where humans and robots coexist harmoniously, supporting and complementing each other in the pursuit of progress and collective well-being.

THIS PAGE INTENTIONALLY LEFT BLANK

Chapter 11: What Happens if Things Go <u>Wrong</u> with Working with Robots?

Working with robots offers a multitude of advantages, but it also comes with its share of challenges and potential pitfalls. In this chapter, we will explore the potential risks and issues that may arise when working with robots, aiming to shed light on the importance of proactive measures, responsible practices, and ongoing vigilance to ensure the safe and ethical integration of robotics in our society.

Safety Hazards and Risks

Robotic systems, if not properly designed, maintained, and controlled, can pose significant safety hazards to humans and the environment. Malfunctioning robots, programming errors, or inadequate safety protocols can lead to accidents, injuries, or property damage. It is crucial to identify and mitigate these risks through robust safety assessments, rigorous testing, and adherence to industry standards and guidelines.

Job Displacement and Economic Implications

The increasing automation and adoption of robots in various industries raise concerns about job displacement and its broader economic implications. As robots take over certain tasks previously performed by humans, it can result in unemployment and economic inequality. Addressing these challenges requires proactive measures such as reskilling programs, job transition support, and policies that foster a balanced workforce ecosystem.

Ethical Dilemmas and Decision-Making

Working with robots raises ethical dilemmas, particularly in scenarios where autonomous systems are entrusted with decision-making. Questions arise regarding the moral framework embedded in robot algorithms, the potential for bias, and the accountability for the outcomes of robot-led decisions. Establishing ethical guidelines, transparency, and oversight mechanisms are essential to navigate these complex ethical considerations.

Social and Psychological Impact

The integration of robots into our daily lives can have a profound impact on social dynamics and psychological well-being. Human-robot interactions may lead to feelings of isolation, displacement, or even dehumanization in certain contexts. Addressing these concerns requires a thoughtful design that considers human needs, fostering a sense of community and belonging, and promoting healthy relationships between humans and robots.

Privacy and Security Concerns

The widespread use of robots equipped with sensors, cameras, and data processing capabilities raises concerns about privacy and security. Unauthorized access, data breaches, or misuse of personal information can result in significant harm to individuals and society. Implementing robust security measures, data protection protocols, and ensuring transparency in data handling are crucial to maintaining trust and safeguarding privacy.

Maintaining Control and Oversight

As robots become more autonomous and capable, ensuring human control and oversight becomes paramount. It is essential to maintain the ability to intervene, override, or stop robotic systems in case of unexpected or undesirable behavior. Establishing clear protocols, fail-safe mechanisms, and maintaining human decision-making authority are critical safeguards in working with robots.

Preparing for Unintended Consequences

Working with robots requires a proactive approach to anticipate and mitigate unintended consequences. Unforeseen circumstances, emergent behaviors, or unforeseen interactions between robots and their environment can have far-reaching implications. Conducting thorough risk assessments, scenario planning, and ongoing monitoring and learning are necessary to respond effectively to these unforeseen challenges.

Research, Collaboration, and Responsibility

To navigate the potential pitfalls of working with robots, interdisciplinary research, collaboration, and shared responsibility are essential. Close collaboration between roboticists, engineers, ethicists, policymakers, and society at large can foster a comprehensive understanding of the risks and challenges. By working together, we can develop strategies and frameworks for the improvement and development of safer and more responsible robotics. This may involve refining regulations, enhancing safety measures, and fostering a culture of responsible robotics. Striving for a balanced and ethical approach to working with robots will contribute to creating a future where humans and machines can coexist harmoniously.

While working with robots offers numerous benefits, it is crucial to acknowledge and address the potential risks and challenges. By proactively identifying safety hazards, addressing ethical dilemmas, safeguarding privacy and security, and maintaining human control, we can navigate the complexities of working with robots. Collaboration, research, and responsible practices are key to ensuring a future where the integration of robots enhances our lives while minimizing unintended consequences.

THIS

PAGE

INTENTIONALLY

LEFT

BLANK

Chapter 12: Can there be a Balance Between Humans and Robots Working Together?

The evolving landscape of human-robot collaboration has opened up new possibilities and challenges. Finding a balance between humans and robots is essential to harness the full potential of this collaboration while ensuring the well-being of both parties. In this chapter, we will explore the dynamics, design principles, ethical considerations, training, psychological implications, policy framework, and case studies that contribute to achieving a harmonious and productive balance in human-robot collaboration.

Understanding the Dynamics of Human-Robot Collaboration

To establish a balance, it is crucial to understand the strengths and limitations of both humans and robots. Humans bring creativity, intuition, and emotional intelligence, while robots offer precision, efficiency, and tireless work ethic.

Recognizing and embracing the complementary nature of human-robot collaboration allows us to leverage the unique capabilities of each party to achieve optimal results.

Designing for Effective Collaboration

Human-centered design principles play a vital role in ensuring effective collaboration between humans and robots. Designing intuitive and adaptable interfaces, considering user feedback and preferences, and incorporating human-centric considerations in robot development are crucial steps. By creating a collaborative environment that supports seamless interaction and communication, we enhance the potential for balance in human-robot collaboration.

Enhancing Trust and Communication

Trust is a cornerstone of successful collaboration. Building trust between humans and robots requires transparency, reliability, and consistency in robot behavior. Effective communication channels, both verbal and non-verbal, play a pivotal role in fostering mutual understanding and ensuring clear instructions and feedback. Establishing trust and open lines of communication contributes to a balanced and harmonious working relationship.

Establishing Ethical Guidelines for Human-Robot Interaction

Ethical considerations are essential when humans and robots collaborate. Developing comprehensive guidelines ensures that robot behaviors align with societal values, human rights, and fairness. It involves addressing questions of responsibility, accountability, privacy, and the impact of robot decisions on human lives. Striking the right balance between autonomy and control in human-robot collaboration is crucial to maintain ethical standards.

Training and Education for Human-Robot Collaboration

To facilitate a balanced collaboration, adequate training programs are necessary for humans working with robots. These programs should cover technical skills, understanding robot capabilities and limitations, and the social and psychological aspects of human-robot interaction. Promoting interdisciplinary education that combines robotics and human sciences fosters a deeper understanding and appreciation of the complexities involved in collaboration.

Psychological and Social Implications of Human-Robot Collaboration

The psychological and social implications of human-robot collaboration should not be overlooked. Understanding the impact on job satisfaction, well-being, and social dynamics is essential for maintaining a healthy work environment.

Addressing social and emotional needs in human-robot interactions, such as companionship and emotional support, helps establish a balanced relationship where both humans and robots thrive.

The Role of Policies and Regulations

Policies and regulations play a crucial role in governing the deployment and use of robots in various domains. They ensure the protection of privacy, safety, and security in human-robot collaboration. Collaborative efforts between policymakers, industry stakeholders, and academia are necessary to establish guidelines that foster a balanced and responsible approach to human-robot collaboration.

Case Studies of Successful Human-Robot Collaboration

Examining real-world examples of successful human-robot collaboration provides valuable insights and best practices. Case studies across industries and domains shed light on the challenges faced, lessons learned, and strategies employed to achieve balance and productivity. Analyzing these cases helps us understand the factors that contribute to successful collaborations and provides guidance for future endeavors.

The Future of Human-Robot Collaboration

Looking ahead, we must anticipate future trends and advancements in robotics that will shape the landscape of human-robot collaboration. Ethical considerations, continued research, technological innovations, and societal feedback will guide the path toward a balanced and mutually beneficial relationship. Embracing a forward-thinking mindset and adapting to changing dynamics will enable us to navigate the complexities of human-robot collaboration successfully.

Achieving a balance between humans and robots working together is a dynamic and ongoing process. By understanding the dynamics of collaboration, designing for effective interaction, establishing ethical guidelines, providing appropriate training and education, addressing psychological and social implications, and implementing thoughtful policies, we can foster a harmonious and productive relationship between humans and robots. The journey towards balance requires continuous learning, adaptation, and a shared commitment to shaping the future of human-robot collaboration.

Chapter 13: The Wildcard: Humankind's Use of Technology for Good or Evil?

Technology has become an integral part of our lives, revolutionizing the way we live, work, and interact. It possesses an inherent duality, capable of bringing immense benefits or causing significant harm. In this chapter, we delve into the unpredictable nature of technology and explore how it has been used for both good and evil.

The Power of Technology

Technological advancements have progressed at an exponential rate, unlocking new possibilities and transforming various industries. The potential of technology knows no bounds, with innovations shaping our future in profound ways. From artificial intelligence and robotics to genetic engineering and nanotechnology, the impact of technology is felt across the globe.

Technology for Good

Harnessing the power of technology, humanity has made remarkable strides in improving our collective well-being. In the realm of healthcare and medicine, technology has revolutionized diagnostics and treatment, leading to more accurate diagnoses and innovative therapies. Surgical procedures have become safer and more precise, while telemedicine and remote healthcare enable access to quality care in remote areas.

Furthermore, technology has emerged as a crucial ally in environmental conservation and sustainability. Renewable energy solutions, such as solar and wind power, have gained prominence, reducing our reliance on fossil fuels. Conservation efforts are aided by advanced monitoring systems, satellite imaging, and data analytics, allowing us to protect fragile ecosystems and combat climate change.

Education and knowledge sharing have also been transformed by technology. Online learning platforms provide opportunities for people worldwide to access education, regardless of geographical constraints. The democratization of information and resources through the internet has bridged educational divides, empowering individuals and fostering lifelong learning.

In times of humanitarian crises and natural disasters, technology plays a vital role in providing aid and support. From remote sensing and mapping to efficient communication and coordination, technology enables rapid response and relief efforts, saving lives and alleviating suffering.

Technology for Evil

However, alongside its immense potential for good, technology presents a dark side that must not be ignored. Cybersecurity threats and data breaches have become rampant, with hackers exploiting vulnerabilities and compromising personal information. The specter of state-sponsored cyberattacks looms large, posing threats to national security and global stability. The protection of personal and sensitive data has become a pressing concern.

Weaponization and autonomous warfare pose ethical dilemmas and potential dangers. Lethal autonomous weapons, capable of making life-or-death decisions without human intervention, raise questions about accountability and the preservation of human dignity. International regulations and arms control frameworks are necessary to mitigate the risks associated with the militarization of technology.

Social and ethical implications also arise from the pervasive use of technology. Privacy concerns are amplified as surveillance technologies become more sophisticated, blurring the boundaries between public and private spheres. Algorithmic biases and discrimination perpetuated by automated systems further exacerbate social inequalities. The digital divide, characterized by unequal access to technology and digital literacy, deepens existing societal disparities.

Striking a Balance

In light of the dual nature of technology, it is imperative to strike a balance between innovation and responsibility. Responsible innovation entails considering the broader societal impact of technological advancements and incorporating ethical considerations throughout the design and implementation process. Ethical frameworks and guidelines can guide the development and deployment of technology in ways that prioritize human well-being and social good.

Collaboration between technology innovators and policymakers is crucial to ensure that regulations keep pace with technological advancements. By fostering dialogue and collaboration, we can establish policies that address emerging challenges and promote responsible technology use.

Engaging the public in technological decision-making processes is equally important, as it ensures diverse perspectives and promotes democratic governance of technology.

As we reflect on the potential of technology, it becomes clear that our responsibility for its use is paramount. Embracing the transformative power of technology requires a proactive approach that puts humanity's best interests at the forefront.

By understanding the potential for good and evil and actively shaping a future where technology serves the greater good, we can navigate the uncertain landscape and create a world where technology enhances our lives while preserving our values.

THIS

PAGE

INTENTIONALLY

LEFT

BLANK

Chapter 14: What Does the Future Hold for AI, Robots, and Humans?

In this pivotal chapter, we embark on a profound exploration of the future implications that AI, robots, and humans hold. Building upon the foundation laid by preceding chapters, we delve into the potential scenarios, challenges, and ethical considerations that lie ahead as these entities continue to coexist and shape our society. As we witness the exponential growth of technological advancements, it becomes increasingly crucial to navigate this complex landscape mindfully, ensuring that we uphold our values and safeguard the collective well-being of humanity.

The Acceleration of Technological Advancements

The rapid pace at which AI and robotics are advancing has transformed countless industries and revolutionized the way we live and work. Breakthroughs in machine learning, deep learning, and robotics have propelled us towards extraordinary achievements. From self-driving cars to advanced natural language processing, these technologies have become integral to our daily lives. Looking ahead, we are on the brink of witnessing even greater advancements, as AI and robots become seamlessly integrated into various domains such as healthcare, transportation, and manufacturing. As the intelligence of AI increases and robots become more sophisticated, we must grapple with the profound societal shifts that await us.

Potential Scenarios for Coexistence

To envision the future of AI, robots, and humans, we must consider the potential scenarios that may unfold. One optimistic scenario is that of collaborative coexistence, where humans and AI/robots work synergistically, combining their unique strengths to enhance productivity and creativity. This partnership has the potential to yield groundbreaking advancements in scientific research, healthcare innovation, and creative endeavors. However, we must also acknowledge the challenges that lie ahead. Job displacement and the subsequent economic implications pose significant concerns as automation progresses. The ethical dimensions of AI and robot decision-making raise important questions that require careful consideration. Furthermore, controversial topics such as AI and robot rights, as well as the nature of consciousness, add layers of complexity to the path forward.

Ethical Frameworks and Regulation

As the impact of AI and robotics expands, it is crucial to establish robust ethical frameworks and regulations. Existing ethical guidelines must be revisited and adapted to effectively address the evolving challenges posed by these technologies. Transparency, accountability, and fairness must be at the forefront of AI development and deployment. Striking a delicate balance between innovation and ethical considerations is paramount to ensure that AI and robots are harnessed for the benefit of humanity. It is through multidisciplinary collaboration among researchers, policymakers, and stakeholders that we can navigate the ethical complexities that lie ahead.

Impact on Different Sectors of Society:

The future of AI, robots, and humans will undoubtedly have a profound impact on various sectors of society. In the field of healthcare and medicine, AI holds the potential to revolutionize diagnosis and treatment, enabling personalized and precise care. Robotic assistance in surgeries can enhance surgical precision, ultimately improving patient outcomes. Nevertheless, ethical considerations regarding data privacy, bias, and human-AI collaboration in healthcare decision-making must be carefully addressed. In the education and workforce sectors, AI-enabled personalized learning has the capacity to cater to individual needs, while reskilling programs will be vital to prepare the workforce for an AI-centric future. Redefining job roles and ensuring a just transition are critical aspects to be considered. Additionally, the emergence of AI companions and social robots will reshape the landscape of relationships and social interactions. Ethical questions surrounding human-robot relationships, consent, and the potential erosion of human connection require thoughtful examination.

Mindful Coexistence: Nurturing the Human Spirit:

As AI and robots become increasingly pervasive, it is imperative that we intentionally cultivate and nurture the human spirit. Fostering human values, emotional intelligence, and empathy will play a vital role in preserving our humanity.

While AI can automate tasks, it cannot replicate the depth and essence of the human experience. Maintaining a sense of purpose, meaning, and connection in a world influenced by AI and robots will require conscious efforts. We must ensure that technological progress aligns with our collective well-being, placing human flourishing at the forefront.

Reflections on the Path Forward:

The future of AI, robots, and humans is not predetermined; it is shaped by our choices and actions. As we navigate this complex terrain, it is crucial to reflect on the path forward.

Spirituality and wisdom can serve as guiding principles, helping us strike a delicate balance between progress and the well-being of humanity. Active engagement in discussions and collaborations, fostering a multi-stakeholder approach that includes individuals, policymakers, and technologists, is key. By cultivating an inclusive and thoughtful dialogue, we can actively shape a future where AI, robots, and humans coexist harmoniously, promoting a society that prioritizes the well-being and flourishing of all.

The future of AI, robots, and humans holds vast promise and significant challenges. The accelerating pace of technological advancements demands our unwavering attention as we contemplate potential scenarios for their coexistence. Establishing ethical frameworks and regulations is imperative to ensure responsible development and deployment of AI and robotics. The impact on different sectors of society necessitates careful planning and consideration of ethical implications. Mindful coexistence, with a focus on nurturing the human spirit, is crucial to preserve our humanity in a world increasingly influenced by AI and robots. By reflecting on the path forward and engaging in thoughtful dialogue, we can actively shape a future where these entities serve as enablers rather than masters, fostering a society that prioritizes the well-being and flourishing of all.

THIS PAGE INTENTIONALLY LEFT BLANK

Conclusion

As we draw near the culmination of our profound exploration into AI, human, and robot interaction, we find ourselves standing at the precipice of a pivotal juncture. Throughout our journey, we have embarked on a quest to unravel the intricate tapestry woven by questions surrounding artificial intelligence, consciousness, self-actualization, sentience, and the quintessence of being human or a robot. Now, as we cast our gaze into the future, we are confronted with a momentous task—the shaping of the destiny that awaits AI, robots, and humanity.

Our odyssey into the depths of AI has revealed the boundless potential it carries, as well as the transformative power it bestows upon us. We have borne witness to its capacity to augment human capabilities, revolutionize industries, and unlock uncharted realms of knowledge. Yet, AI transcends the mere realm of technology, for it serves as the bridge that spans the chasm between what is and what could be - a catalyst that ignites innovation and propels us toward unparalleled progress.

Consciousness, that enigmatic essence that defines our subjective experience, has served as a lynchpin in our pursuit of understanding. While AI has demonstrated remarkable feats of intelligence, the true nature of consciousness remains an elusive mystery, evading replication within the confines of algorithms and circuits. Our human existence is imbued with emotions, motivations, and desires, shaping our experiences and guiding our decisions. To be a self-actualized being is to embark upon a personal odyssey of growth, fulfillment, and the actualization of our unique potential. It is a voyage of self-discovery, introspection, and alignment with our true purpose.

Sentience, the capacity to perceive and experience the world, delineates us as beings endowed with empathy, compassion, and interconnectedness. In our exploration of sentience, we have unearthed the significance of nurturing our human spirit—the wellspring of our capacity to love, create, and empathize. In contrast, robots, though imbued with intelligence, lack the innate sentience that underpins human experiences. They are the offspring of human ingenuity, engineered to fulfill specific functions and tasks with precision and efficiency.

Through the juxtaposition of humans and robots, we have unveiled both similarities and disparities. We share a common pursuit of progress, a collective yearning to enhance our lives and transform our world. Nevertheless, it is our imperfections, the intangible fabric of our humanity, that distinguishes us. Our humanity lies in our ability to navigate uncertainty, to adapt, and evolve. Robots, on the other hand, embody precision, reliability, and the unparalleled processing power to analyze vast troves of data. As we traverse the path of coexistence, embracing and understanding these distinctive qualities becomes paramount.

The impact of robots upon our lives is multifold. They possess the potential to increase productivity, enhance healthcare, and revolutionize myriad industries. Yet, their integration also kindles legitimate concerns, ranging from job displacement to ethical considerations and the preservation of our human essence. When our collaboration with robots thrives, we bear witness to heightened efficiency, collaborative synergies, and the realization of remarkable achievements. However, when the delicate balance falters, we face the perils of unintended consequences, ethical quandaries, and the erosion of genuine human connection.

The future we envision hinges upon striking a harmonious balance between humans and robots. It is a delicate equilibrium that demands collaboration, dialogue, and the establishment of robust ethical frameworks. By forging a symbiotic relationship—one that harnesses the unique strengths of both humans and robots—we can cultivate a coexistence that amplifies human potential and serves the greater good of society. This equilibrium necessitates proactive measures to mitigate risks, prioritize the well-being of all, and ensure that technology remains a benevolent enabler rather than a tyrant.

Amidst the vast array of possibilities, we acknowledge the wildcard of humankind's utilization of technology—a force that can be wielded for either benevolence or malevolence. Technology, when wielded responsibly and consciously, possesses the potential to uplift and empower. However, when misused or driven by malicious intent, it can lead to grave consequences. Thus, it is our collective responsibility to harness technology for the betterment of humanity—a future where AI and robots coexist in harmony, infused with compassion, empathy, and wisdom.

As we cast our gaze toward the future, the question of what lies ahead for AI, robots, and humans looms large. The answer rests within our choices, actions, and aspirations. By adopting an inclusive, multidisciplinary approach—engaging individuals, policymakers, and technologists—we can actively mold a future in which AI and robots serve as instruments of human progress. We must infuse the realms of science and technology with the essence of spirituality, ethics, and humanity, ensuring that the well-being and flourishing of all beings remain at the forefront of our endeavors.

In the end, the coexistence of AI, robots, and humans transcends the realm of technological endeavor—it is a profound spiritual odyssey. It beckons us to reflect upon our essence, values, and the legacy we wish to leave behind. It is an opportunity to shape a future that seamlessly harmonizes technological progress with the preservation of our humanity.

As we embark upon this transformative path, let us remember that the future we envision lies within our grasp—awaiting our conscious choices and collective actions. Together, we can embrace coexistence, transcend boundaries, and forge a future that celebrates the profound beauty of our shared existence.

THIS PAGE INTENTIONALLY LEFT BLANK

Bibliography

Chapter 1: Exploring AI, Human, and Robot Interaction

Introduction:

- Floridi, L. (2019). The Fourth Revolution: How the Infosphere is Reshaping Human Reality. Oxford University Press. (Book)
- Harari, Y. N. (2018). 21 Lessons for the 21st Century. Spiegel & Grau. (Book)

Section 1: Understanding AI and Robotics

Definition and Scope of Artificial Intelligence

- Russell, S., & Norvig, P. (2016). Artificial Intelligence: A Modern Approach (3rd ed.). Pearson. (Book)
- McCarthy, J., Minsky, M. L., Rochester, N., & Shannon, C. E. (1955). A Proposal for the Dartmouth Summer Research Project on Artificial Intelligence. AI Magazine, 27(4), 12-14. (Journal article)

The Nature of Robotics

- Murphy, R. R. (2000). Introduction to AI Robotics. MIT Press. (Book)
- Brooks, R. A. (1991). Intelligence Without Representation. Artificial Intelligence, 47(1-3), 139-159. (Journal article)

Section 2: The Human Experience

Unique Human Qualities

- Damasio, A. (1999). The Feeling of What Happens: Body and Emotion in the Making of Consciousness. Harcourt. (Book)
- Gazzaniga, M. S. (2011). Who's in Charge?: Free Will and the Science of the Brain. Ecco. (Book)

Human Potential and Limitations

- Csikszentmihalyi, M. (1997). Finding Flow: The Psychology of Engagement with Everyday Life. Basic Books. (Book)
- Pinker, S. (2002). The Blank Slate: The Modern Denial of Human Nature. Penguin Books. (Book)

Section 3: Interaction Dynamics

Collaborative Efforts: Humans and Robots Working Together

- Feil-Seifer, D., & Matarić, M. J. (2011). Robots for Use in Autism Research. Annual Review of Biomedical Engineering, 13, 275-294. (Journal article)
- Zhang, J., Gombolay, M., & Knepper, R. A. (2018). A Computational Model for Task Switching in Human-Robot Collaboration. Robotics and Autonomous Systems, 99, 170-184. (Journal article)

Human-Robot Interface and Communication

- Fong, T., Nourbakhsh, I., & Dautenhahn, K. (2003). A Survey of Socially Interactive Robots. Robotics and Autonomous Systems, 42(3-4), 143-166. (Journal article)
- Goodrich, M. A., & Schultz, A. C. (2007). Human-Robot Interaction: A Survey. Foundations and Trends in Human-Computer Interaction, 1(3), 203-275. (Journal article)

Section 4: Ethical and Social Implications

Ethics in AI and Robotics

- Bostrom, N. (2014). Superintelligence: Paths, Dangers, Strategies. Oxford University Press. (Book)
- Calo, R. (2017). Artificial Intelligence Policy: A Primer and Roadmap. SSRN Electronic Journal. (Journal article)

Societal Impact

- Brynjolfsson, E., & McAfee, A. (2016). The Second Machine

Age: Work, Progress, and Prosperity in a Time of Brilliant Technologies. W. W. Norton & Company. (Book)
- Acemoglu, D., & Restrepo, P. (2020). Robots and Jobs: Evidence from US Labor Markets. Journal of Political Economy, 128(6), 2188-2244. (Journal article)

Section 5: The Spiritual Perspective

Consciousness and Technology

- Damasio, Antonio. "The Feeling of What Happens: Body and Emotion in the Making of Consciousness."
- Schneider, Susan. "Consciousness in the Age of Artificial Intelligence."

Transcending Dualism

- Grof, Stanislav. "The Holotropic Mind: The Three Levels of Human Consciousness and How They Shape Our Lives."
- Warwick, Kevin, and Huma Shah. "Artificial Intelligence and the Reenchantment of the World."

Technology as a Tool for Spiritual Growth

- Smith, Ethan Indigo. "The Technology of Spirituality: Reaching Through the Veil of Death."
- Klestinec, Cynthia. "The Spiritual Potential of Robotics: The Promise and the Peril."

Section 6: The Path to Harmonious Coexistence

Ethical Guidelines for AI and Robotics

- IEEE Global Initiative for Ethical Considerations in Artificial Intelligence and Autonomous Systems. "Ethically Aligned Design: A Vision for Prioritizing Human Well-being with Artificial Intelligence and Autonomous Systems."
- Müller, Vincent C. "Ethics of Artificial Intelligence and Robotics."

Cultivating Digital Mindfulness

- Newport, Cal. "Digital Minimalism: Choosing a Focused Life in a Noisy World."
- Seibt, Peter, and Bernhard Humm. "Digital Mindfulness: Mindfulness in the Age of Complexity."

Section 7: Implications for Work and Education

Transforming the Work Landscape

Brynjolfsson, Erik, McAfee, Andrew. "The Second Machine Age: Work, Progress, and Prosperity in a Time of Brilliant Technologies."

Frey, Carl Benedikt, Osborne, Michael A. "The Future of Employment: How Susceptible Are Jobs to Computerization?" (Oxford Martin School, University of Oxford).

Education for the Future

- Zhao, Yong. "World Class Learners: Educating Creative and Entrepreneurial Students."
- Wagner, Tony. "The Global Achievement Gap: Why Even Our Best Schools Don't Teach the New Survival Skills Our Children Need—and What We Can Do About It."

Section 8: Cultivating Ethical AI and Responsible Development

Ethical Considerations in AI Design

- Mittelstadt, Brent Daniel, et al. "The Ethics of Algorithms: Mapping the Debate." (Big Data & Society journal)
- Jobin, Anna, Ienca, Marcello, Vayena, Effy. "The Global Landscape of AI Ethics Guidelines." (Nature Machine Intelligence journal)

Responsible Deployment of AI and Robots

- Floridi, Luciano. "The Ethics of Artificial Intelligence." (Stanford Encyclopedia of Philosophy)
- Brundage, Miles, et al. "The Malicious Use of Artificial

Intelligence: Forecasting, Prevention, and Mitigation." (arXiv preprint)

Chapter 2: What is AI (Artificial Intelligence)?

Historical Development of AI:

- "The History of Artificial Intelligence" by Computer History Museum: https://www.computerhistory.org/timeline/artificial-intelligence/
- "A Brief History of Artificial Intelligence" by Alan Turing Institute: https://www.turing.ac.uk/blog/brief-history-artificial-intelligence

Types of AI:

- "Narrow AI vs. General AI: What's the Difference?" by Investopedia: https://www.investopedia.com/terms/a/artificial-intelligence-ai.asp
- "What is General AI (Artificial General Intelligence)?" by Towards Data Science: https://towardsdatascience.com/what-is-general-ai-artificial-general-intelligence-73a9f3ad2d5e

Core Components of AI Systems:

- "Machine Learning: A Probabilistic Perspective" by Kevin P. Murphy (book)
- "Natural Language Processing with Python" by Steven Bird, Ewan Klein, and Edward Loper (book)
- "Computer Vision: Algorithms and Applications" by Richard Szeliski (book)

Ethical Considerations in AI:

- "Ethics of Artificial Intelligence and Robotics" by Stanford Encyclopedia of Philosophy: https://plato.stanford.edu/entries/ethics-ai/
- "Fairness and Bias in Machine Learning" by Microsoft Research: https://www.microsoft.com/en-us/research/project/fairness-accountability-transparency-and-ethics-in-ai/

- "The Malicious Use of Artificial Intelligence: Forecasting, Prevention, and Mitigation" by Brundage et al. (research paper): https://arxiv.org/abs/1802.07228

Challenges and Limitations of AI:

- "Artificial Intelligence as Structural Estimation: Economic Interpretations of Deep Blue, Bonanza, and AlphaGo" by Susan Athey (research paper): https://web.stanford.edu/~athey/beta4.pdf
- "The Limitations of AI in Contextual Understanding" by Medium: https://medium.com/towards-artificial-intelligence/the-limitations-of-ai-in-contextual-understanding-71f13467b7e9
- The Intersection of AI with Other Fields:
- "Artificial Intelligence in Healthcare: Anticipating Challenges to Ethics and Privacy" by David Leslie (research paper): https://pubmed.ncbi.nlm.nih.gov/27484347/
- "AI in Finance: 10 Current Applications" by Emerj: https://emerj.com/ai-sector-overviews/ai-in-finance/

Future Directions of AI:

- "The Future of Artificial Intelligence: Where Do We Go from Here?" by Medium: https://medium.com/swlh/the-future-of-artificial-intelligence-where-do-we-go-from-here-76b3706c74b6
- "AI Now 2020 Report" by AI Now Institute: https://ainowinstitute.org/AI_Now_2020_Report.pdf

Chapter 3: What is Consciousness?

Introduction to Consciousness:

- Blackmore, S. (2004). Consciousness: An Introduction. Oxford University Press.
- Dennett, D. C. (1991). Consciousness Explained. Back Bay Books.

The Nature of Consciousness:

- Chalmers, D. (1995). Facing up to the problem of consciousness. Journal of Consciousness Studies, 2(3), 200-219.
- Penrose, R. (1989). The Emperor's New Mind: Concerning Computers, Minds, and the Laws of Physics. Oxford University Press.
- Tononi, G. (2008). Consciousness as Integrated Information: A Provisional Manifesto. Biological Bulletin, 215(3), 216-242.

Consciousness in AI and Robots:

- Kurzweil, R. (2005). The Singularity is Near: When Humans Transcend Biology. Penguin Books.
- Bostrom, N. (2014). Superintelligence: Paths, Dangers, Strategies. Oxford University Press.
- Searle, J. R. (1997). The Mystery of Consciousness. Granta Books.

Consciousness and Spiritual Perspectives:

- Deikman, A. J. (1982). The Observing Self: Mysticism and Psychotherapy. Beacon Press.
- Tarnas, R. (2006). Cosmos and Psyche: Intimations of a New World View. Plume.

The Human-Technology Relationship:

- Harari, Y. N. (2015). Homo Deus: A Brief History of Tomorrow. Harper.

- Kabat-Zinn, J. (1994). Wherever You Go, There You Are: Mindfulness Meditation in Everyday Life. Hyperion.

Coexistence and Co-creation:

- Koch, C. (2012). Consciousness: Confessions of a Romantic Reductionist. The MIT Press.
- Metzinger, T. (Ed.). (2000). Neural Correlates of Consciousness: Empirical and Conceptual Questions. MIT Press.

Chapter 4: What does it Mean to be a Self-Actualized Being?

Introduction to Self-Actualization:

- Maslow, A. H. (1954). Motivation and Personality. Harper.

The Characteristics of a Self-Actualized Being:

- Maslow, A. H. (1970). Motivation and Personality (2nd ed.). Harper & Row.

- Deci, E. L., & Ryan, R. M. (2000). Self-Determination Theory and the Facilitation of Intrinsic Motivation, Social Development, and Well-Being. American Psychologist, 55(1), 68-78.

Self-Actualization and Inner Transformation:

- Brown, B. (2012). Daring Greatly: How the Courage to Be Vulnerable Transforms the Way We Live, Love, Parent, and Lead. Avery.

- Neff, K. D. (2011). Self-Compassion: Stop Beating Yourself Up and Leave Insecurity Behind. William Morrow.

Self-Actualization and Purpose:

- Frankl, V. E. (2006). Man's Search for Meaning. Beacon Press.

- Dik, B. J., & Duffy, R. D. (2009). Calling and Vocation at Work: Definitions and Prospects for Research and Practice. The Counseling Psychologist, 37(3), 424-450.

Self-Actualization and Relationships:

- Rogers, C. R. (1961). On Becoming a Person: A Therapist's View of Psychotherapy. Houghton Mifflin.

- Goleman, D. (2006). Social Intelligence: The New Science of Human Relationships. Bantam.

Self-Actualization and Mindfulness:

- Kabat-Zinn, J. (1994). Wherever You Go, There You Are:

Mindfulness Meditation in Everyday Life. Hachette Books.
- Salzberg, S. (2011). Real Happiness: The Power of Meditation: A 28-Day Program. Workman Publishing.

Self-Actualization and Spirituality:
- Tolle, E. (2004). The Power of Now: A Guide to Spiritual Enlightenment. New World Library.
- Wilber, K. (2000). Integral Psychology: Consciousness, Spirit, Psychology, Therapy. Shambhala.

Obstacles and Challenges on the Path to Self-Actualization:
- Csikszentmihalyi, M. (1991). Flow: The Psychology of Optimal Experience. Harper Perennial.
- Dweck, C. (2006). Mindset: The New Psychology of Success. Ballantine Books.

Cultivating Self-Actualization in the Technological Age:
- Harris, T. (2019). Digital Minimalism: Choosing a Focused Life in a Noisy World. Portfolio.
- Newport, C. (2016). Deep Work: Rules for Focused Success in a Distracted World. Grand Central Publishing.

Chapter 5: What does it Mean to be a Sentient Being?

Introduction to Sentience:

- "Consciousness Explained" by Daniel C. Dennett
- "The Feeling of What Happens: Body and Emotion in the Making of Consciousness" by Antonio Damasio

The Nature of Sentience:

- "The Conscious Mind: In Search of a Fundamental Theory" by David J. Chalmers
- "Consciousness: An Introduction" by Susan Blackmore

Cognitive and Emotional Aspects of Sentience:

- "Emotional Intelligence: Why It Can Matter More Than IQ" by Daniel Goleman
- "The Self Illusion: How the Social Brain Creates Identity" by Bruce Hood

Ethical Implications of Sentience:

- "Animal Liberation: The Definitive Classic of the Animal Movement" by Peter Singer
- "Ethics into Action: Henry Spira and the Animal Rights Movement" by Peter Singer

Sentience and the Human-Technology Relationship:

- "Alone Together: Why We Expect More from Technology and Less from Each Other" by Sherry Turkle
- "The Emotion Machine: Commonsense Thinking, Artificial Intelligence, and the Future of the Human Mind" by Marvin Minsky

The Quest for Artificial Sentience:

- "Superintelligence: Paths, Dangers, Strategies" by Nick Bostrom
- "Life 3.0: Being Human in the Age of Artificial Intelligence" by Max Tegmark

Philosophical Perspectives on Sentience:
- "Consciousness and the Brain: Deciphering How the Brain Codes Our Thoughts" by Stanislas Dehaene
- "The Conscious Mind: A Philosophical Road Trip" by David J. Chalmers

The Future of Sentience:
- "Homo Deus: A Brief History of Tomorrow" by Yuval Noah Harari
- "Robot Ethics: The Ethical and Social Implications of Robotics" edited by Patrick Lin, Keith Abney, and George A. Bekey

Chapter 6: What Does it Mean to Be Human?

Section 1: The Essence of Humanity

Human Identity:

- Book: "Consciousness Explained" by Daniel C. Dennett.
- Article: "What Makes Us Conscious?" by Christof Koch (Scientific American).
- Research paper: "The Moral Brain: A Multidisciplinary Perspective" by Jorge Moll et al. (Nature Reviews Neuroscience).

The Human Experience:

- Book: "Emotional Intelligence" by Daniel Goleman.
- Article: "The Science of Empathy" by Tania Singer and Olga M. Klimecki (The American Scientist).
- Research paper: "The Neural Bases of Social Cognition and Story Comprehension" by Roberta A. Adolphs (Annual Review of Psychology).

Section 2: Differentiating Humans from AI and Robots

The Limitations of AI and Robots:

- Book: "Artificial Intelligence: A Modern Approach" by Stuart Russell and Peter Norvig.
- Article: "Limits of Artificial Intelligence" by Rodney Brooks (MIT Technology Review).
- Research paper: "The Artificial Intelligence Fallacy" by Gary Marcus (Medium).

Human Creativity and Ingenuity:

- Book: "The Innovator's Dilemma" by Clayton M. Christensen.
- Article: "The Nature of Human Creativity" by Robert J. Sternberg (Creativity Research Journal).
- Research paper: "Creativity and the Brain: Recent Advances" by Rex E. Jung et al. (Current Opinion in

Behavioral Sciences).

Section 3: Ethical and Moral Considerations

Ethical Frameworks:

- Book: "Ethics for the Information Age" by Michael J. Quinn.
- Article: "The Ethics of Artificial Intelligence" by Nick Bostrom and Eliezer Yudkowsky (Cambridge Handbook of Artificial Intelligence).
- Research paper: "Towards Ethical Guidelines for Decentralized Robotics" by Mark Coeckelbergh (Ethics and Information Technology).

Moral Agency and Responsibility:

- Book: "Moral Machines: Teaching Robots Right from Wrong" by Wendell Wallach and Colin Allen.
- Article: "The Challenge of Moral Responsibility for Intelligent Systems" by Vincent C. Müller (Science and Engineering Ethics).
- Research paper: "Responsibility and the Moral Phenomenology of Human-Robot Interaction" by Shannon Vallor (Ethics and Information Technology).

Chapter 7: What Does it Mean to Be a Robot?

Section 1: The Nature of Robotics

- "Introduction to Robotics: Mechanics and Control" by John J. Craig
- "Robotics: Modelling, Planning, and Control" by Bruno Siciliano and Lorenzo Sciavicco
- "Robotics: A Very Short Introduction" by Alan Winfield
- "Robotics: Science and Systems" (Conference Proceedings)

Section 2: Intelligence and Autonomy in Robots

- "Artificial Intelligence: A Modern Approach" by Stuart Russell and Peter Norvig
- "Deep Learning" by Ian Goodfellow, Yoshua Bengio, and Aaron Courville
- "Reinforcement Learning: An Introduction" by Richard S. Sutton and Andrew G. Barto
- "Autonomous Robots: From Biological Inspiration to Implementation and Control" by George A. Bekey

Section 3: Ethical and Moral Considerations

- "Robot Ethics: The Ethical and Social Implications of Robotics" edited by Patrick Lin, Keith Abney, and George A. Bekey
- "Machine Ethics" by Michael Anderson and Susan Leigh Anderson
- "Robot Rights" by David J. Gunkel
- "Ethics of Artificial Intelligence and Robotics" (Stanford Encyclopedia of Philosophy)

Section 4: Coexistence and Collaboration between Humans and Robots

- "Human-Robot Interaction" by Cynthia L. Breazeal
- "Social Robotics: An Interdisciplinary Approach" edited by

Giuseppe F. Italiano and Angelo Cangelosi
- "The Second Machine Age: Work, Progress, and Prosperity in a Time of Brilliant Technologies" by Erik Brynjolfsson and Andrew McAfee
- "Robot-Proof: Higher Education in the Age of Artificial Intelligence" by Joseph E. Aoun

Chapter 8: Comparing Humans to Robots – The Similarities and Differences

Section 1: Physical Characteristics

Human Anatomy:

- Book: "Human Anatomy" by Frederic H. Martini and Robert B. Tallitsch
- Scientific Journal: "The Anatomy and Physiology of the Human Body" by Henry Gray

Robot Design:

- Book: "Robotics: Modelling, Planning and Control" by Bruno Siciliano and Lorenzo Sciavicco
- Scientific Journal: "Design Principles for Robotic Systems" by Rodney A. Brooks

Section 2: Cognitive Abilities

Human Intelligence:

- Book: "Intelligence: From Secrets to Policy" by Mark M. Lowenthal
- Scientific Journal: "The Cognitive Neuroscience of Human Intelligence: A Review" by Richard J. Haier

Artificial Intelligence in Robots:

- Book: "Artificial Intelligence: A Modern Approach" by Stuart Russell and Peter Norvig
- Scientific Journal: "Artificial Intelligence in Robotics: A Review" by Sebastian Thrun and Wolfram Burgard

Section 3: Emotional and Social Dimensions

Human Emotions:

- Book: "Emotions: A Brief History" by Felipe De Brigard
- Scientific Journal: "The Science of Emotion: Research and Tradition in the Psychology of Emotion" by Richard S. Lazarus

Robot Emotion and Social Interaction:

- Book: "Social Robotics: Second International Conference, ICSR 2010" edited by Vanessa Evers, et al.
- Scientific Journal: "Emotional Robotics in Social Human-Robot Interaction: A Review" by Cynthia Breazeal

Section 4: Ethical and Moral Considerations

Moral Agency and Responsibility:

- Book: "Moral Responsibility" by David Shoemaker
- Scientific Journal: "Moral Responsibility and Determinism: The Cognitive Science of Folk Intuitions" by Shaun Nichols and Joshua Knobe

Ethical Implications of Human-Robot Interactions:

- Book: "Robot Ethics: The Ethical and Social Implications of Robotics" by Patrick Lin, et al.
- Scientific Journal: "Ethical Considerations in Human-Robot Interaction" by Alan R. Wagner and Noel Sharkey

Section 5: Societal Impact and Future Perspectives

- Impact on Employment and Economy:
- Book: "The Future of Work: Robots, AI, and Automation" by Darrell M. West
- Scientific Journal: "The Impact of Robots on Employment, Wages, and Productivity" by Georg Graetz and Guy Michaels

Coexistence and Collaboration:

- Book: "The Second Machine Age: Work, Progress, and Prosperity in a Time of Brilliant Technologies" by Erik Brynjolfsson and Andrew McAfee
- Scientific Journal: "Collaborative Human-Robot Interaction: The State of the Art and the Future Challenges" by Bilge Mutlu and Wendy A. Kellogg

Chapter 9: Robots – Are They Helping Us or Hurting Us?

The Benefits of Robots:

- Brynjolfsson, Erik, and McAfee, Andrew. "The Second Machine Age: Work, Progress, and Prosperity in a Time of Brilliant Technologies."

The Challenges Posed by Robots:

- Aoun, Joseph E. "Robot-Proof: Higher Education in the Age of Artificial Intelligence."
- Kaplan, Jerry. "Humans Need Not Apply: A Guide to Wealth and Work in the Age of Artificial Intelligence."
- Lin, Patrick, Abney, Keith, and Bekey, George A. (Editors). "Robot Ethics: The Ethical and Social Implications of Robotics."

The Impact on Social Dynamics:

- Mindell, David A. "Our Robots, Ourselves: Robotics and the Myths of Autonomy."
- Calo, Ryan, Froomkin, A. Michael, and Kerr, Ian (Editors). "Robot Law."

Finding the Balance: Human-Robot Collaboration:

- Reese, Byron. "The Fourth Age: Smart Robots, Conscious Computers, and the Future of Humanity."

Ethical Considerations and Regulation:

- Lin, Patrick, Abney, Keith, and Bekey, George A. (Editors). "Robot Ethics: The Ethical and Social Implications of Robotics."
- Calo, Ryan, Froomkin, A. Michael, and Kerr, Ian (Editors). "Robot Law."

The Spiritual Perspective (Philosophical and spiritual literature exploring consciousness, interconnectedness, and personal growth provided relevant perspectives):

- Watts, Alan. "The Book: On the Taboo Against Knowing Who You Are."
- Tolle, Eckhart. "The Power of Now: A Guide to Spiritual Enlightenment."
- Chopra, Deepak. "The Book of Secrets: Unlocking the Hidden Dimensions of Your Life."
- Singer, Michael A. "The Untethered Soul: The Journey Beyond Yourself."
- Wilber, Ken. "The Essential Ken Wilber: An Introductory Reader."
- Hesse, Hermann. "Siddhartha."
- Dass, Ram. "Be Here Now."
- Harari, Yuval Noah. "Sapiens: A Brief History of Humankind."

Chapter 10: What Happens if Things Go <u>Right</u> with Working with Robots?

Introduction:

Bostrom, N. (2014). Superintelligence: Paths, Dangers, Strategies. Oxford University Press.

Enhancing Efficiency and Productivity:

- Brynjolfsson, E., & McAfee, A. (2014). The Second Machine Age: Work, Progress, and Prosperity in a Time of Brilliant Technologies. W. W. Norton & Company.
- McAfee, A., & Brynjolfsson, E. (2017). Machine, Platform, Crowd: Harnessing Our Digital Future. W. W. Norton & Company.

Empowering Human Potential:

- Pink, D. H. (2009). Drive: The Surprising Truth About What Motivates Us. Riverhead Books.
- Davenport, T. H., & Kirby, J. (2015). Only Humans Need Apply: Winners and Losers in the Age of Smart Machines. HarperBusiness.

Transforming Industries and Driving Innovation:

- West, J., & Bogers, M. (2017). Digital Innovation: The Interplay of Sociotechnical Networks in a Digital World. Oxford University Press.
- McAfee, A., & Brynjolfsson, E. (2016). Machine, Platform, Crowd: Harnessing Our Digital Future. W. W. Norton & Company.

Improving Quality of Life:

- Topol, E. (2019). Deep Medicine: How Artificial Intelligence Can Make Healthcare Human Again. Basic Books.
- Coghlan, D., & Brennan, L. (2017). Robot-Proof: Higher Education in the Age of Artificial Intelligence. MIT Press.

Advancing Scientific Frontiers:
- Lee, M. (2015). Architects of Intelligence: The Truth About AI from the People Building It. Packt Publishing.
- Russell, S. J., & Norvig, P. (2016). Artificial Intelligence: A Modern Approach. Pearson.

Fostering Collaboration and Cultural Exchange:
- Benkler, Y. (2017). The Wealth of Networks: How Social Production Transforms Markets and Freedom. Yale University Press.
- Floridi, L. (2019). The Fourth Revolution: How the Infosphere Is Reshaping Human Reality. Oxford University Press.

Conclusion:
- Harris, S. (2016). The Moral Landscape: How Science Can Determine Human Values. Free Press.
- Harari, Y. N. (2018). 21 Lessons for the 21st Century. Spiegel & Grau.

Chapter 11: What Happens if Things Go <u>Wrong</u> with Working with Robots?

1. Safety Hazards and Risks

- Robot Safety Standards and Guidelines: International Organization for Standardization (ISO)
Website: https://www.iso.org/standards.html
- Leveson, N. G. (2012). Engineering a Safer World: Systems Thinking Applied to Safety. MIT Press.

Rethinking Robotics Safety: Collaboration between Industry and Academia

- Article by McDermid, J. et al. (2017)
Available at: https://ieeexplore.ieee.org/document/8010732

2. Job Displacement and Economic Implications

- Brynjolfsson, E., & McAfee, A. (2014). The Second Machine Age: Work, Progress, and Prosperity in a Time of Brilliant Technologies. W. W. Norton & Company.
- Autor, D. H. (2015). Why Are There Still So Many Jobs? The History and Future of Workplace Automation. Journal of Economic Perspectives, 29(3), 3-30.
- Future of Work: Robotics, Artificial Intelligence, and Automation
Report by the Pew Research Center (2014)
Available at: https://www.pewresearch.org/internet/2014/08/06/future-of-jobs/

3. Ethical Dilemmas and Decision-Making

- Floridi, L. (2014). The Fourth Revolution: How the Infosphere is Reshaping Human Reality. Oxford University Press.
- Bostrom, N. (2014). Superintelligence: Paths, Dangers, Strategies. Oxford University Press.

- Johnson, D. G., & Powers, T. M. (2008). Computer Systems: Ethical and Social Implications. Pearson.

4. Social and Psychological Impact
- Turkle, S. (2011). Alone Together: Why We Expect More from Technology and Less from Each Other. Basic Books.
- Shneiderman, B. (2015). The New ABCs of Research: Achieving Breakthrough Collaborations. Oxford University Press.
- Reeves, B., & Nass, C. (1996). The Media Equation: How People Treat Computers, Television, and New Media Like Real People and Places. Cambridge University Press.

5. Privacy and Security Concerns
- Cavoukian, A. (2011). Privacy by Design: The 7 Foundational Principles. Information and Privacy Commissioner of Ontario, Canada.
- Clarke, R., & Wigan, M. R. (2011). You Can't Opt Out of Privacy: A Case Study of the Myki Card. Computer Law & Security Review, 27(1), 26-43.
- Solove, D. J. (2013). Nothing to Hide: The False Tradeoff Between Privacy and Security. Yale University Press.

6. Maintaining Control and Oversight
- Winfield, A. F. (2018). Human Autonomy and Responsibility in the Age of Autonomous Systems. Science and Engineering Ethics, 24(2), 399-414.
- Wallach, W., & Allen, C. (2009). Moral Machines: Teaching Robots Right from Wrong. Oxford University Press.
- Calo, R. (2017). The Case for a Federal Robotics Commission. In SSRN Electronic Journal.

7. Preparing for Unintended Consequences
- Sullins, J. P. (2016). When Is a Robot a Moral Agent?

International Journal of Technoethics, 7(2), 1-16.

- Future of Artificial Intelligence: OpenAI Charter

Available at: https://www.openai.com/charter/

- Johnson, D. G. (2016). Robot Ethics. In Zalta, E. N. (Ed.), The Stanford Encyclopedia of Philosophy.

Available at:

https://plato.stanford.edu/archives/win2016/entries/ethics-robot/

Chapter 12: Can there be a Balance between Humans and Robots Working Together?

1. Introduction

- Floridi, L. (2019). The Logic of Information: A Theory of Philosophy as Conceptual Design. Oxford University Press.
- Bostrom, N. (2014). Superintelligence: Paths, Dangers, Strategies. Oxford University Press.

2. Understanding the Dynamics of Human-Robot Collaboration

- Breazeal, C. (2002). Designing Sociable Robots. MIT Press.
- Turkle, S. (2011). Alone Together: Why We Expect More from Technology and Less from Each Other. Basic Books.

3. Designing for Effective Collaboration

- Norman, D. A. (2013). The Design of Everyday Things. Basic Books.
- Preece, J., Rogers, Y., & Sharp, H. (2019). Interaction Design: Beyond Human-Computer Interaction. John Wiley & Sons.

4. Enhancing Trust and Communication

- Lee, M. K. (2018). Designing for Trust: Four Perspectives and a Research Agenda for Explainable AI User Experiences. Proceedings of the 2018 CHI Conference on Human Factors in Computing Systems.
- Mutlu, B., Forlizzi, J., & Hodgins, J. (2006). A storytelling robot: Modeling and evaluation of human-like gaze behavior. In Proceedings of the 1st ACM SIGCHI/SIGART conference on Human-robot interaction.

5. Establishing Ethical Guidelines for Human-Robot Interaction

- Veruggio, G., Operto, F., & Bekey, G. A. (2009). Roboethics:

A Bottom-up Interdisciplinary Discourse in the Field of Applied Ethics in Robotics. In Roboethics: A Navigating Overview (pp. 29-49). Ios Press.

- Calo, R. (2015). Robotics and the Lessons of Cyberlaw. California Law Review, 103(3), 513-563.

6. Training and Education for Human-Robot Collaboration

- Goodrich, M. A., & Schultz, A. C. (2007). Human-Robot Interaction: A Survey. Foundations and Trends® in Human-Computer Interaction, 1(3), 203-275.

- Johnson, M., & Christensen, H. I. (2016). Robot-Assisted Therapy: A Critical Review of the Current State of the Field. Journal of Rehabilitation and Assistive Technologies Engineering, 3, 2055668316635924.

7. Psychological and Social Implications of Human-Robot Collaboration

- Turkle, S. (2015). Reclaiming Conversation: The Power of Talk in a Digital Age. Penguin Books.

- Bailenson, J. N. (2018). Experience on Demand: What Virtual Reality Is, How It Works, and What It Can Do. WW Norton & Company.

8. The Role of Policies and Regulations

- Bryson, J. J. (2018). Robots Should Be Slaves. In Philosophy of Artificial Intelligence (pp. 229-242). Oxford University Press.

- European Commission. (2020). Ethics Guidelines for Trustworthy AI. Retrieved from https://ec.europa.eu/digital-single-market/en/news/ethics-guidelines-trustworthy-ai

9. Case Studies of Successful Human-Robot Collaboration

- Salge, C., Fisher, M., & Wörgötter, F. (2014). Case studies in robotics and automation. Springer.

- Riek, L. D. (2017). Healthcare robotics. Communications of the ACM, 60(11), 68-78.

10. The Future of Human-Robot Collaboration

- Russell, S., & Norvig, P. (2016). Artificial Intelligence: A Modern Approach. Pearson.

- Shneiderman, B. (2017). Human-Centered Artificial Intelligence: Reliable, Safe & Trustworthy. Policy Brief, One Hundred Year Study on Artificial Intelligence, Stanford University.

Chapter 13: The Wildcard: Humankind's Use of Technology for Good or Evil?

Introduction:

- Floridi, L. (2014). The fourth revolution: How the infosphere is reshaping human reality. Oxford University Press.
- Winner, L. (1980). Do artifacts have politics? Daedalus, 109(1), 121-136.

The Power of Technology:

- Brynjolfsson, E., & McAfee, A. (2014). The second machine age: Work, progress, and prosperity in a time of brilliant technologies. W. W. Norton & Company.
- Kelly, K. (2016). The inevitable: Understanding the 12 technological forces that will shape our future. Penguin.
- Kurzweil, R. (2005). The singularity is near: When humans transcend biology. Penguin.

Technology for Good:

- Topol, E. J. (2019). Deep medicine: How artificial intelligence can make healthcare human again. Basic Books.
- Rifkin, J. (2014). The zero marginal cost society: The internet of things, the collaborative commons, and the eclipse of capitalism. St. Martin's Press.
- Shirky, C. (2010). Cognitive surplus: Creativity and generosity in a connected age. Penguin Books.

Technology for Evil:

- Clarke, R. A., & Knake, R. K. (2012). Cyber war: The next threat to national security and what to do about it. Ecco.
- Scharre, P. W. (2018). Army of none: Autonomous weapons and the future of war. W. W. Norton & Company.
- Zuboff, S. (2019). The age of surveillance capitalism: The fight for a human future at the new frontier of power.

PublicAffairs.

Striking a Balance:

- Floridi, L. (2019). The ethics of information. Oxford University Press.

- Johnson, D. G. (2016). The ethical challenges of emerging technologies. Oxford University Press.

- Ryan, M. D. (2018). Taking the high road: A guide to ethical decision-making in autonomous systems. Artech House.

Chapter 14: What Does the Future Hold for AI, Robots, and Humans?

The Acceleration of Technological Advancements

- Kurzweil, Ray. "The Singularity Is Near: When Humans Transcend Biology." Penguin Books, 2006.

Potential Scenarios for Coexistence

- Bostrom, Nick. "Superintelligence: Paths, Dangers, Strategies." Oxford University Press, 2014.
- Russell, Stuart, and Norvig, Peter. "Artificial Intelligence: A Modern Approach." Pearson, 2016.
- Floridi, Luciano. "The Fourth Revolution: How the Infosphere is Reshaping Human Reality." Oxford University Press, 2014.

Ethical Frameworks and Regulation

- Johnson, Deborah G., and Wetmore, Jameson M. "The Ethics of AI Ethics: An Evaluation of Guidelines." Minds and Machines, vol. 30, no. 1, 2020, pp. 99-120.
- Calo, Ryan. "Robotics and the Lessons of Cyberlaw." California Law Review, vol. 103, no. 3, 2015, pp. 513-564.
- Allen, Colin, and Wallach, Wendell. "Moral Machines: Teaching Robots Right from Wrong." Oxford University Press, 2009.

Impact on Different Sectors of Society

- Topol, Eric. "Deep Medicine: How Artificial Intelligence Can Make Healthcare Human Again." Basic Books, 2019.
- Brynjolfsson, Erik, and McAfee, Andrew. "The Second Machine Age: Work, Progress, and Prosperity in a Time of Brilliant Technologies." W. W. Norton & Company, 2016.
- Turkle, Sherry. "Alone Together: Why We Expect More from Technology and Less from Each Other." Basic Books, 2011.

Mindful Coexistence: Nurturing the Human Spirit

- Harari, Yuval Noah. "21 Lessons for the 21st Century." Spiegel & Grau, 2018.

- Epstein, Robert. "The Case Against Artificial Intelligence: How AI Can Put Your Mind at Ease." Wiley, 2019.

Reflections on the Path Forward

- Dreyfus, Hubert L. "What Computers Still Can't Do: A Critique of Artificial Reason." MIT Press, 1992.

- Rifkin, Jeremy. "The Zero Marginal Cost Society: The Internet of Things, the Collaborative Commons, and the Eclipse of Capitalism." St. Martin's Griffin, 2015.

THIS PAGE INTENTIONALLY LEFT BLANK

Suggested Reading List

Chapter 1: Exploring AI, Human, and Robot Interaction:

- "Superintelligence: Paths, Dangers, Strategies" by Nick Bostrom
- "Human + Machine: Reimagining Work in the Age of AI" by Paul R. Daugherty and H. James Wilson
- "Robot-Proof: Higher Education in the Age of Artificial Intelligence" by Joseph E. Aoun
- "The Second Machine Age: Work, Progress, and Prosperity in a Time of Brilliant Technologies" by Erik Brynjolfsson and Andrew McAfee
- "Artificial Intelligence: A Modern Approach" by Stuart Russell and Peter Norvig
- "Machines of Loving Grace: The Quest for Common Ground Between Humans and Robots" by John Markoff
- "Our Final Invention: Artificial Intelligence and the End of the Human Era" by James Barrat
- "The Age of Spiritual Machines: When Computers Exceed Human Intelligence" by Ray Kurzweil
- "The Sentient Machine: The Coming Age of Artificial Intelligence" by Amir Husain
- "AI Superpowers: China, Silicon Valley, and the New World Order" by Kai-Fu Lee
- "The Industries of the Future" by Alec Ross
- "Robot Ethics: The Ethical and Social Implications of Robotics" edited by Patrick Lin, George Bekey, and Keith Abney

Chapter 2. What is AI (Artificial Intelligence)?

- "Artificial Intelligence: A Modern Approach" by Stuart Russell and Peter Norvig
- "Superintelligence: Paths, Dangers, Strategies" by Nick Bostrom
- "The Master Algorithm: How the Quest for the Ultimate Learning Machine Will Remake Our World" by Pedro Domingos
- "Life 3.0: Being Human in the Age of Artificial Intelligence" by Max Tegmark
- "AI Superpowers: China, Silicon Valley, and the New World Order" by Kai-Fu Lee
- "The AI Delusion" by Gary Smith
- "Human Compatible: Artificial Intelligence and the Problem of Control" by Stuart Russell
- "The Fourth Age: Smart Robots, Conscious Computers, and the Future of Humanity" by Byron Reese
- "Architects of Intelligence: The Truth About AI from the People Building It" edited by Martin Ford
- "The Future of Humanity: Terraforming Mars, Interstellar Travel, Immortality, and Our Destiny Beyond Earth" by Michio Kaku

Chapter 3. What is Consciousness?

- "Consciousness: An Introduction" by Susan Blackmore
"Consciousness Explained" by Daniel C. Dennett
"The Emperor's New Mind: Concerning Computers, Minds, and the Laws of Physics" by Roger Penrose
"The Singularity is Near: When Humans Transcend Biology" by Ray Kurzweil
"Superintelligence: Paths, Dangers, Strategies" by Nick Bostrom
"The Mystery of Consciousness" by John R. Searle
"The Observing Self: Mysticism and Psychotherapy" by Arthur J. Deikman
"Cosmos and Psyche: Intimations of a New World View" by Richard Tarnas
"Homo Deus: A Brief History of Tomorrow" by Yuval Noah Harari
"Wherever You Go, There You Are: Mindfulness Meditation in Everyday Life" by Jon Kabat-Zinn
"Consciousness: Confessions of a Romantic Reductionist" by Christof Koch
"Neural Correlates of Consciousness: Empirical and Conceptual Questions" edited by Thomas Metzinger

Chapter 4. What does it Mean to be a Self-Actualized Being?

- "Motivation and Personality" by Abraham H. Maslow
- "Man's Search for Meaning" by Viktor E. Frankl
- "Daring Greatly: How the Courage to Be Vulnerable Transforms the Way We Live, Love, Parent, and Lead" by Brené Brown
- "Flow: The Psychology of Optimal Experience" by Mihaly Csikszentmihalyi
- "The Power of Now: A Guide to Spiritual Enlightenment" by Eckhart Tolle
- "Self-Compassion: Stop Beating Yourself Up and Leave Insecurity Behind" by Kristin Neff
- "Social Intelligence: The New Science of Human Relationships" by Daniel Goleman
- "Mindset: The New Psychology of Success" by Carol S. Dweck
- "Wherever You Go, There You Are: Mindfulness Meditation in Everyday Life" by Jon Kabat-Zinn
- "Digital Minimalism: Choosing a Focused Life in a Noisy World" by Cal Newport

Chapter 5. What does it Mean to be a Sentient Being?

- "Consciousness Explained" by Daniel C. Dennett
- "The Feeling of What Happens: Body and Emotion in the Making of Consciousness" by Antonio Damasio
- "The Conscious Mind: In Search of a Fundamental Theory" by David J. Chalmers
- "Consciousness: An Introduction" by Susan Blackmore
- "Emotional Intelligence: Why It Can Matter More Than IQ" by Daniel Goleman
- "The Self Illusion: How the Social Brain Creates Identity" by Bruce Hood
- "Animal Liberation: The Definitive Classic of the Animal Movement" by Peter Singer
- "Ethics into Action: Henry Spira and the Animal Rights Movement" by Peter Singer
- "Alone Together: Why We Expect More from Technology and Less from Each Other" by Sherry Turkle
- "The Emotion Machine: Commonsense Thinking, Artificial Intelligence, and the Future of the Human Mind" by Marvin Minsky
- "Superintelligence: Paths, Dangers, Strategies" by Nick Bostrom
- "Life 3.0: Being Human in the Age of Artificial Intelligence" by Max Tegmark
- "Consciousness and the Brain: Deciphering How the Brain Codes Our Thoughts" by Stanislas Dehaene
- "The Conscious Mind: A Philosophical Road Trip" by David J. Chalmers
- "Homo Deus: A Brief History of Tomorrow" by Yuval Noah Harari

- "Robot Ethics: The Ethical and Social Implications of Robotics" edited by Patrick Lin, Keith Abney, and George A. Bekey

Chapter 6. What Does it Mean to Be Human?

- "Consciousness Explained" by Daniel C. Dennett
- "Emotional Intelligence" by Daniel Goleman
- "Artificial Intelligence: A Modern Approach" by Stuart Russell and Peter Norvig
- "The Innovator's Dilemma" by Clayton M. Christensen
- "Ethics for the Information Age" by Michael J. Quinn
- "Moral Machines: Teaching Robots Right from Wrong" by Wendell Wallach and Colin Allen
- "The Second Machine Age: Work, Progress, and Prosperity in a Time of Brilliant Technologies" by Erik Brynjolfsson and Andrew McAfee
- "Homo Deus: A Brief History of Tomorrow" by Yuval Noah Harari

Chapter 7. What Does it Mean to Be a Robot?

- "Introduction to Robotics: Mechanics and Control" by John J. Craig
- "Robotics: Modelling, Planning, and Control" by Bruno Siciliano and Lorenzo Sciavicco
- "Robotics: A Very Short Introduction" by Alan Winfield
- "Artificial Intelligence: A Modern Approach" by Stuart Russell and Peter Norvig
- "Deep Learning" by Ian Goodfellow, Yoshua Bengio, and Aaron Courville
- "Reinforcement Learning: An Introduction" by Richard S. Sutton and Andrew G. Barto
- "Robot Ethics: The Ethical and Social Implications of Robotics" edited by Patrick Lin, Keith Abney, and George A. Bekey
- "Machine Ethics" by Michael Anderson and Susan Leigh Anderson
- "Human-Robot Interaction" by Cynthia L. Breazeal
- "Social Robotics: An Interdisciplinary Approach" edited by Giuseppe F. Italiano and Angelo Cangelosi

Chapter 8. Comparing Humans to Robots – The Similarities and Differences

- "The Age of Spiritual Machines: When Computers Exceed Human Intelligence" by Ray Kurzweil
- "Robot-Proof: Higher Education in the Age of Artificial Intelligence" by Joseph E. Aoun
- "The Emotion Machine: Commonsense Thinking, Artificial Intelligence, and the Future of the Human Mind" by Marvin Minsky
- "Superintelligence: Paths, Dangers, Strategies" by Nick Bostrom
- "Robot Ethics: The Ethical and Social Implications of Robotics" edited by Patrick Lin, Keith Abney, and George A. Bekey
- "Our Robots, Ourselves: Robotics and the Myths of Autonomy" by David A. Mindell
- "The Sentient Machine: The Coming Age of Artificial Intelligence" by Amir Husain
- "Robot Law" edited by Ryan Calo, A. Michael Froomkin, and Ian Kerr
- "Humans Need Not Apply: A Guide to Wealth and Work in the Age of Artificial Intelligence" by Jerry Kaplan
- "The Fourth Age: Smart Robots, Conscious Computers, and the Future of Humanity" by Byron Reese

Chapter 9. Robots – Are They Helping Us or Hurting Us?

- "The Second Machine Age: Work, Progress, and Prosperity in a Time of Brilliant Technologies" by Erik Brynjolfsson and Andrew McAfee.
- "Robot-Proof: Higher Education in the Age of Artificial Intelligence" by Joseph E. Aoun.
- "Humans Need Not Apply: A Guide to Wealth and Work in the Age of Artificial Intelligence" by Jerry Kaplan.
- "Robot Ethics: The Ethical and Social Implications of Robotics" edited by Patrick Lin, Keith Abney, and George A. Bekey.
- "Our Robots, Ourselves: Robotics and the Myths of Autonomy" by David A. Mindell.
- "Robot Law" by Ryan Calo, A. Michael Froomkin, and Ian Kerr (Editors).
- "The Fourth Age: Smart Robots, Conscious Computers, and the Future of Humanity" by Byron Reese.

Chapter 10. What Happens if Things Go Right with Working with Robots?

- "The Second Machine Age: Work, Progress, and Prosperity in a Time of Brilliant Technologies" by Erik Brynjolfsson and Andrew McAfee
- "Machine, Platform, Crowd: Harnessing Our Digital Future" by Andrew McAfee and Erik Brynjolfsson
- "Only Humans Need Apply: Winners and Losers in the Age of Smart Machines" by Thomas H. Davenport and Julia Kirby
- "Drive: The Surprising Truth About What Motivates Us" by Daniel H. Pink
- "Deep Medicine: How Artificial Intelligence Can Make Healthcare Human Again" by Eric Topol
- "Robot-Proof: Higher Education in the Age of Artificial Intelligence" by Joseph E. Aoun
- "Architects of Intelligence: The Truth About AI from the People Building It" by Martin Ford
- "Artificial Intelligence: A Modern Approach" by Stuart Russell and Peter Norvig
- "The Wealth of Networks: How Social Production Transforms Markets and Freedom" by Yochai Benkler
- "The Fourth Revolution: How the Infosphere Is Reshaping Human Reality" by Luciano Floridi
- "The Moral Landscape: How Science Can Determine Human Values" by Sam Harris
- "21 Lessons for the 21st Century" by Yuval Noah Harari

Chapter 11. What Happens if Things Go Wrong with Working with Robots?

- "Robot-Proof: Higher Education in the Age of Artificial Intelligence" by Joseph E. Aoun
- "The Rise of the Robots: Technology and the Threat of a Jobless Future" by Martin Ford
- "Our Robots, Ourselves: Robotics and the Myths of Autonomy" by David A. Mindell
- "Robot Ethics: The Ethical and Social Implications of Robotics" edited by Patrick Lin, Keith Abney, and George A. Bekey
- "The Sentient Machine: The Coming Age of Artificial Intelligence" by Amir Husain
- "Robot Law" by Ryan Calo, A. Michael Froomkin, and Ian Kerr
- "Moral Machines: Teaching Robots Right from Wrong" by Wendell Wallach and Colin Allen
- "Robot Rules: Regulating Artificial Intelligence" by Jacob Turner
- "The Fourth Age: Smart Robots, Conscious Computers, and the Future of Humanity" by Byron Reese
- "Ethics of Artificial Intelligence and Robotics" edited by Vincent C. Müller

Chapter 12. Can there be a Balance between Humans and Robots Working Together?

- "The Second Machine Age: Work, Progress, and Prosperity in a Time of Brilliant Technologies" by Erik Brynjolfsson and Andrew McAfee
- "The Future of Work: Robots, AI, and Automation" by Darrell M. West
- "Our Robots, Ourselves: Robotics and the Myths of Autonomy" by David A. Mindell
- "The Rise of the Robots: Technology and the Threat of Mass Unemployment" by Martin Ford
- "The Fourth Industrial Revolution" by Klaus Schwab
- "Robot-Proof: Higher Education in the Age of Artificial Intelligence" by Joseph E. Aoun
- "Humans Need Not Apply: A Guide to Wealth and Work in the Age of Artificial Intelligence" by Jerry Kaplan
- "The Robots Are Coming!: The Future of Jobs in the Age of Automation" by Andres Oppenheimer
- "Machine, Platform, Crowd: Harnessing Our Digital Future" by Andrew McAfee and Erik Brynjolfsson
- "The Inevitable: Understanding the 12 Technological Forces That Will Shape Our Future" by Kevin Kelly

Chapter 13. The Wildcard: Humankind's Use of Technology for Good or Evil?

- "The Shallows: What the Internet Is Doing to Our Brains" by Nicholas Carr
- "Weapons of Math Destruction: How Big Data Increases Inequality and Threatens Democracy" by Cathy O'Neil
- "The Fourth Industrial Revolution" by Klaus Schwab
- "The Future of the Mind: The Scientific Quest to Understand, Enhance, and Empower the Mind" by Michio Kaku
- "Superintelligence: Paths, Dangers, Strategies" by Nick Bostrom
- "Surveillance Valley: The Secret Military History of the Internet" by Yasha Levine
- "The Age of Surveillance Capitalism: The Fight for a Human Future at the New Frontier of Power" by Shoshana Zuboff
- "The Innovators: How a Group of Hackers, Geniuses, and Geeks Created the Digital Revolution" by Walter Isaacson
- "Homo Deus: A Brief History of Tomorrow" by Yuval Noah Harari
- "The Code Book: The Science of Secrecy from Ancient Egypt to Quantum Cryptography" by Simon Singh

Chapter 14. What Does the Future Hold for AI, Robots, and Humans?

- "The Singularity Is Near: When Humans Transcend Biology" by Ray Kurzweil
- "Artificial Intelligence: A Modern Approach" by Stuart Russell and Peter Norvig
- "The Fourth Revolution: How the Infosphere is Reshaping Human Reality" by Luciano Floridi
- "Robot Ethics: The Ethical and Social Implications of Robotics" edited by Patrick Lin, Keith Abney, and George A. Bekey
- "Machine, Platform, Crowd: Harnessing Our Digital Future" by Andrew McAfee and Erik Brynjolfsson
- "Deep Medicine: How Artificial Intelligence Can Make Healthcare Human Again" by Eric Topol
- "The Age of Em: Work, Love, and Life when Robots Rule the Earth" by Robin Hanson
- "Human Compatible: Artificial Intelligence and the Problem of Control" by Stuart Russell
- "The Second Machine Age: Work, Progress, and Prosperity in a Time of Brilliant Technologies" by Erik Brynjolfsson and Andrew McAfee
- "21 Lessons for the 21st Century" by Yuval Noah Harari
- "The Case Against Artificial Intelligence: How AI Can Put Your Mind at Ease" by Robert Epstein
- "The Future of Humanity: Terraforming Mars, Interstellar Travel, Immortality, and Our Destiny Beyond Earth" by Michio Kaku
- "The Rise of Robots: Technology and the Threat of a Jobless Future" by Martin Ford

- "The Industries of the Future" by Alec Ross

NOTES

NOTES